*Why Does God
Permit Evil?*

Dom Bruno Webb

Why Does God Permit Evil?

SOPHIA INSTITUTE PRESS®
Manchester, New Hampshire

Why Does God Permit Evil? was originally published by P. J. Kenedy and Sons, New York, in 1941. This 2004 edition by Sophia Institute Press® contains minor editorial revisions to the original text.

Copyright © 2004 Sophia Institute Press®

Printed in the United States of America

All rights reserved

Cover design by Theodore Schluenderfritz

Sophia Institute Press®
Box 5284, Manchester, NH 03108
1-800-888-9344
www.sophiainstitute.com

Imprimi potest: Dom Wilfrid Upson, O.S.B., Abbot of Prinknash
December 29, 1940
Nihil obstat: Henry F. Davis, Censor Deputatus
Imprimatur: Thomas, Archbishop of Birmingham

Library of Congress Cataloging-in-Publication Data

Webb, Bruno.
    Why does God permit evil? / Bruno Webb.
        p. cm.
    Originally published: London : Burns, Oates & Washbourne, 1941.
        ISBN 1-928832-76-8 (pbk. : alk. paper)
        1. Good and evil. 2. Suffering. I. Title.
BJ1408.W4
2004 231′.8 — dc22   2004006477

Contents

Editor's note: The biblical quotations in the following pages are taken from the Douay-Rheims edition of the Old and New Testaments. Where applicable, quotations have been cross-referenced with the differing names and enumeration in the Revised Standard Version, using the following symbol: (RSV =).

*

Foreword

At the dawn of reason, we became conscious of "the riddle of the painful earth," and the riddle grows more complicated as we advance in years.

Every system of philosophy, every religion that has ever existed from the dawn of creation down to the present day, has had to face the problem of evil in its manifold guises. Diverse ethical systems have sprung from the various solutions offered.

Countless volumes have been written on this vexing problem from the philosophical and theological standpoints, mostly discussing the nature and origin of evil.

With regard to the nature of evil, there is pretty general agreement that it is not "a thing in itself," but rather a condition, a privation of being; or, as St. Thomas Aquinas has it, "the deficiency of some good which ought to be present."[1] But when we come to consider the origin of evil, we are well-nigh deafened by the din of contending parties. Dualistic systems such as Zoroastrianism and Manicheanism dramatized the problem, but left it unexplained and so soon gave way to monistic interpretations of various kinds, theistic, atheistic, and agnostic, ranging in tone from rosy optimism to the depths of pessimism.

It must be confessed that most treatises on the problem of evil make very dull reading, but this little book by Dom Bruno Webb, O.S.B., is a marked exception. It is at once arresting, refreshing, stimulating, and comforting. Needless to say, it is informing, but Dom Bruno is little concerned with metaphysical speculation, and is less taken up with the nature and origin of evil than with its *function*. He makes it clear that evil has a function that gives it a meaning and a place in the theodicy of the Christian religion. He interprets evil in the light of the two great doctrines of the solidarity of the human race and of the Mystical Body of Christ. Here again it is not his purpose to enter into an academic exposition of these doctrines, but

[1] St. Thomas Aquinas (1225-1274; Dominican philosopher, theologian, and Doctor), *Summa Theologica*, I-II, Q. 49, art. 1.

rather to consider them in their actual workings and in their correlations with the everyday life of the Christian.

This book offers a practical message to the stricken, the sorrowful, and the suffering, and to all who strive to bring themselves into union with Christ crucified, the Head of the Mystical Body, of which we are the members. We wish this volume the wide circulation it certainly deserves.

The Most Reverend Richard Downey,
D.D., Ph.D., LL.D.,
Archbishop of Liverpool

✳

Author's Note

The following essay does not set out to examine every question connected with the subject of evil, but to deal with the main problem by presenting the answer given to us by revelation as we find it set forth by the Church, and primarily in her Liturgy.

It seeks also to be practical, since it is of little use to know why God has permitted suffering unless we know also how to deal with it in our own lives.

I therefore offer this little essay with the hope that, by God's blessing, it may serve to bring peace of soul to some on whom, especially in these troubled days, the yoke of suffering weighs heavily — such peace as the world can neither give nor take away, that peace which, on the night of Christ's birth, was promised to all those who sincerely seek God:

Why Does God Permit Evil?

"Glory to God in the highest, and on earth peace to men of good will."[2]

Dom Bruno Webb, O.S.B.
Abbey of St. Mary and St. Peter,
Prinknash, Gloucester,
Birthday of Our Lord Jesus Christ 1940

[2] Luke 2:14.

❧

Why Does God
Permit Evil?

✻

Sin causes all evil

The existence of evil, at all times a difficult problem, is especially so in this largely neopagan century to those who have had but little chance of studying the principles of sound truth. Whether it be moral evil — that is to say, sin — or physical evil, of which the most evident form is suffering, the fact faces us at every turn. Not one of us escapes it, and for many it is a crushing and overwhelming one. The dilemma of Epicurus is repeated by thousands today: "Omnipotence could, Benevolence would have prevented evil." If God exists, why does He permit injustice, tyranny, war, disease, oppression of the poor, and all the evils that beset our race? In every age, the human mind, unaided by revelation, has tried to solve this problem. A few prominent examples will serve to show with what result.

Why Does God Permit Evil?

※

For many, escape is the response to suffering

The Buddha said, "The origin of suffering is the thirst for existence," that evil is inherent in the very fact of existence, and by our desire to continue our personal existence, we remain enmeshed in the suffering involved by existence as a fly in a spider's web. To escape suffering, we must live devoid of all desire even to exist, or else we shall pay for it by reincarnation in another body to live our suffering life anew. Only by rejecting our very desire for existence can we attain to Nirvana, which, so far as one can understand the Eastern mind, is either loss of personal existence or an eternal unconscious repose. The highest end, therefore, we can attain is negative, and the only way to deal with suffering is by escape.

The Stoics, whose watchword was *duty*, advocated a lofty independence and superiority to the events of life, a proud, stern aloofness that forbade even grief for the loss of friends. They steeled themselves indeed to endure suffering, they professed great disdain for it, and yet by the very fact of thus reducing their passions to the coldness of steel, they sought not to feel it. They had no *use* for suffering; it was something to avoid, and no more. Once again, theirs was a philosophy of escape.

Their contemporaries the Epicureans started from the opposite extreme — namely, pleasure — yet they sought the same end. Temporal pleasure is the supreme good, the desire of immortality must be eradicated — pleasure bodily and mental, but carefully moderated, for excess brings its reaction in pain.

If we turn to neopaganism, we may take the example of Nietzsche. Here we find a new form of escape — namely, defiance. Christianity is a slave morality, cultivating such cringing virtues as humility and compassion. We have to cultivate a "master morality," "a race of supermen," and "the weak must go to the wall." Crush out suffering, for yourself, although by no means for others, by defiance and brute force. Significantly, this prophet of the superman ended his days by going out of his mind. Yet, in strange contrast with his own philosophy, which had condemned the weak as unworthy to live, he accepted, during the years of his own weakness, the care and protection of his aged mother.

This was the philosophy of Berlin, which, with its cult of the Nordic Blood, regarded nations other than its own as worthy only to be slave nations and, with its gospel of sterilization, sent the weak to the wall. Insofar as it advocated defiance, it was also in effect the philosophy of

Why Does God Permit Evil?

Moscow, although in some respects so different and even opposed to that of Berlin, its Marxist slogan being that "religion is the opiate of the people," since it "drugs" man into resignation to life's sufferings, instead of rousing him to defiance and revolt by whatever means.

And apart from any philosophy such as these, it is true that many will endure great suffering for the sake of ambition. But this is because the evil of one is outweighed by the good of the other. Such as these make no pretense to a philosophy that regards suffering as something in any way precious in itself, for as soon as they are faced with suffering that leads to no temporal good, whether ambition, wealth, or pleasure, escape proves to be their only resource. How often it has happened that a man has endured even intense hardship either for the ambition of his "honor" or for wealth or power, yet, when his "honor" is lost through some humiliation, or his wealth or power through some unsuccessful deal, he has shot himself. Hardship was outweighed by "honor," but for the agony of humiliation there was no compensation, and no remedy save the escape, or rather the supposed escape, of suicide.

The attitude of pagan philosophy, then, is, first, that suffering, not sin, is the supreme evil; and, second, that the only means of dealing with suffering is escape, of any kind and as complete as possible. Methods differ. But whether it be the avoidance of all desire, stoic indifference, carefully moderated pleasure, or defiance, the end is the same: escape.

"I often think," says Fr. Vincent McNabb, O.P., "the world's amusements are a sign of despair. [The world] is running away from something. People are clutching at certain things from despair. . . . The soul can easily be stampeded in a crisis. The world is being stampeded now."

We are threatened with legalized euthanasia. If sin does not exist, and if suffering is the supreme evil, why should a person go on enduring the agonies of cancer when there is no hope of recovery? That is the one attitude.

The other is that of the old mother who refused morphine in her dying agonies, so that with her last breath she might wrest from God the conversion of her prodigal. Between these two a gulf is fixed. The world may not know it, but the world is on the run, seeking escape. By *peace* it means the absence of suffering; therefore, it never finds peace.

The peace of Christ is completely different, for on Calvary profound peace and unspeakable suffering were welded into one. To this mystery of suffering, grace alone — that is to say, the supernatural light given to us by revelation — gives a sane answer. Man's reason, by its merely natural power, has failed.

A child cannot understand why his mother sometimes insists on giving him such nasty medicines, because his mind is too undeveloped to grasp the reasons that are so clear to her. Yet what is the difference between the understanding of a child and that of his mother when compared with the difference between man's very limited understanding and the infinite wisdom of God? The answer that revelation gives to this problem of suffering is one wholly surpassing anything that unaided reason has so much as dreamed of.

Nietzsche said, "Cease to look beyond the stars for your hopes and rewards." It is precisely because the Church has her Head, who is Christ, in Heaven, and from that high vantage point can survey the entire situation, that she alone can give a sane answer to the demands of reason. The Church, with her Head above the stars, sees, with a light that comes from God, the meaning of things that take place under the stars. On the underside of a canvas of needlework stretched on a frame can be seen nothing but a jumble of meaningless tags of silk, yet she who works from above sees the design as it develops in all its clearness.

❧

Sin is the origin of evil

The Catholic theology of evil is condensed in the parable of the Prodigal Son.[3] First came sin, a moral evil — that is to say, an evil arising from the abuse of man's free will. From sin followed suffering, a physical evil, as its natural and inevitable effect. But, finally, the last state of the prodigal was better than the first, since from his suffering was drawn a good far greater than that which he originally possessed.

First, then, came sin; that is the origin of all evil. And if, as revelation tells us, all sins, and the first of all sins — namely, the sin of Lucifer — imply the rejection of the supernatural gift of grace, it is a foregone conclusion that merely natural reason, that is to say, pure philosophy, although great use of it is made in dealing with this problem of evil, cannot by itself present us with the ultimate solution, since pure philosophy as such makes no claim to know anything of the supernatural.

Many people have only a vague notion of what sin is. They see the pain and distress that is in the world; they are stirred by the injustices of man against man, of class

[3] Luke 15:11-32.

against class, and of nation against nation. The world understands sin against one's fellowmen, but it is far slower to understand sin against God. We hear much today of the rights of free peoples and the honor of nations, but how much of the rights and the honor of God? Sin is the one supreme evil in the world. It is the evil from which all other evils eventually flow; indeed it is the only evil that ultimately matters at all, for while all other evils, our earthly suffering included, end with time, sin can continue into the world to come as an everlasting separation of the soul from God.

Yet even this is not the principal reason why sin is the supreme evil. The evil of sin consists in its being the fully willful rejection of God; it is, as it were, an attempt to annihilate God, and, were this possible, it would do so. Sin is in a sense an infinite evil, because it is an outrage against the infinite sanctity and goodness of God. It is only insofar as we understand who God is that we can understand what sin is; it is only insofar as we realize that God is the one supreme Reality that we can realize that sin is the one supreme evil; and it is only insofar as we understand that sin is the one supreme evil that we shall understand those other and far lesser evils in the world, suffering in particular, that flow eventually from sin.

ᴪ

God raises man to
share in His divine life

Another all-important reality for us to understand before going further is that of sanctifying grace, that is to say, the supernatural life to which God has raised both angels and men, for sin implies also the rejection of this. The word *nature* in its widest sense is synonymous with created being, whether angelic or human. The supernatural, since it is that which is above the natural, is also that which is above all created being whatsoever, and above even all possible created being; that is to say, it is uncreated Being. God alone is supernatural Being, because He is uncreated, infinite, and eternal. Yet God's plan in creation is that He should leave neither angel nor man in a merely natural state. He created them in order to raise them to the supernatural state. But if God is the only supernatural Being, what does it mean to raise natural and created beings to the supernatural state? It means that, in some way, God raises angels and men to share in *His own divine Life*, as St. Peter says in his second letter, to become "partakers of the divine nature."[4]

[4] 2 Pet. 1:4.

Why Does God Permit Evil?

How can God raise a mere creature to share in His own uncreated life? We will help ourselves out with an analogy. Imagine a number of pieces of wax, each of a different color: blue, green, red, and so on. Someone has a seal bearing the royal arms, and with this seal, he imprints onto each of these pieces of wax the impress of the royal arms. What is the result? In a sense, each of these pieces of wax, whatever its color, has become royal; it bears the king's arms and is raised above its mere nature as wax into the sphere of royalty. If any of us received a letter with the royal arms on the sealing-wax, we would value that piece of wax, not because it was wax, but because of its royal impress. It would be worth any number of wax pieces on which the arms had not been printed.

Now, the pieces of wax represent created beings; all have that in common. The color of each piece of wax represents the particular nature of each created being, for there are countless angels, each of which is a distinct nature, and there is man with his own distinctive human nature. There is but one seal from which are derived all the impressions on the wax, however many they may be, and the seal represents God Himself. Just as the seal imprints its own royal impress upon the pieces of wax, so God imprints His own divine impress upon the angels and the souls of men, thus raising them to the divine sphere as the seal raises the wax pieces to the royal sphere, so that all created beings that possess understanding and free will — namely, angels and men — are raised to partake in God's own life, which is supernatural because it is infinitely above all natural or created being. As the wax pieces become royal, so do angels and men become divine — not, of course, by substantial identity with God any more than the wax becomes identified substantially with the king himself, but by an accidental union so close that the divine life permeates their whole beings through and through, enabling them literally to live by the supernatural life of God Himself, to understand and see with His own supernatural vision, and to love with His own infinite and burning supernatural love.

The analogy of the wax and seal falls immeasurably short of this tremendous mystery which it seeks to put into simple and familiar language such as we can understand; no analogy can do more than this when used to illustrate what is fully understood by God alone. When one analogy fails in part to represent the truth, often the use of a number of analogies throws more light, and in this case, it may help us to understand how the creature, whether angelic or human, is transformed by being permeated by the life of God through all its being, if we think of the difference between a piece of cold iron that we can handle and touch and the same piece of iron hissing and spluttering in the white heat of the furnace; or again, of a wire or cable the moment before and the moment after it makes contact with its dynamo, at one moment lifeless, at the next infused with a power so great that it can drive trains, light up cities, and transform itself indefinitely according to the needs of man. Does the wire look any different when charged with its current? No, by looking at it, you could not tell the difference, yet how different it really is!

Neither can we now see the difference between a person who is in the state of sanctifying grace and one who is not — not, that is to say, so long as we remain on earth; but in Heaven, when grace has fructified into glory, and when angels and the souls of men will be directly visible to the eyes of our intellects as material things are now visible to our material eyes, we shall see the difference. Then, for the first time, we shall understand what is meant by God raising us to partake in His own supernatural life.

Sanctifying grace, then, which is the partaking by each creature in the one divine life of God, differs from God Himself as the impress of the seal in the wax differs from the seal itself. This will give some idea of what sanctifying grace is. It remains, of course, in great measure a mystery — how could it be otherwise when the tiny mind of man is dealing with the infinite Being of God? — yet by revealed light, we know this much of the truth, and it has been necessary to explain it here if we are to understand what is to follow.

The end to which our elevation to the supernatural state leads is the eternal face-to-face vision of God. It is this that constitutes the essential bliss of Heaven. Were man in the state of pure nature, the vision of God would be impossible; the most that men could hope for would be a merely natural happiness in the next life that would consist in no more than an indirect knowledge of God through the medium of created things; we would never be able to see Him face-to-face. The reason is this: between any faculty and its object there must be proportion. For instance, no animal can read a book, because it is limited to mere sense faculties and has no understanding. But God, who is the object of the soul's vision in Heaven, is infinite, and between the soul's finite faculty and this infinite object, there is an infinite lack of proportion. But by being raised to the supernatural state, men and angels come to share in God's *own life*, so that in Heaven they see God Himself by partaking in *God's own vision of Himself*, a vision that consists in the soul's being permeated through and through with the unveiled Being of God. It is this sharing in God's own uncreated life that ravishes and intoxicates the soul with a bliss that is beyond anything we can conceive of now.

꙳

Man is both an individual and
a member of an organic unity

With this digression, we may return to the parable of the Prodigal Son. The prodigal may be taken to represent the entire human race as a unity in itself, as a single organism with Adam as its source and fountainhead. God has made us human beings, not merely as individuals, but as members of a single organic whole, the human race. We are no less truly members of this organic unity, of a *single* race that is organically one because derived from a single origin, than we are distinct individuals. The minds of many people today are set in a subjective and individualistic mold, and they regard man as though he were a mere individual and no more. They realize indeed that he is a social being, and that he depends for most things in life upon cooperation with his fellowmen, yet they regard the human race as though it were no more than a collection of individuals. This is to understand only one side of man's nature, leaving the other side of his nature wholly out of consideration. It is therefore a failure to understand what the nature of man really is.

In actual fact, the social character of man is the sign and the outcome of something much more radical. For man bears a twofold character: he is truly an individual, but he is no less truly a *member* of a higher unity. In the scheme of creation, the entire human race as such is truly a single thing, as objectively real a unity as each individual man is. This is more than a social unity; it is an organic unity that can by analogy be compared to the organic unity of the human body, which is made up of many distinct members or organs, each of which, in turn, is made up of thousands of microscopic cells, and each of these members and cells shares in the welfare of the body as a whole, whether for good or for ill.

For instance, the human eye has a certain individuality of its own, yet it is made to exist and function only as a member or organic part of the human body as such. So far is this true that the eye, although in a sense an individual thing in itself, is altogether incapable of existing as an individual apart from its membership in the body, since it would then cease to be an eye at all and would become instead a mere lump of putrid matter incapable of functioning and devoid of life. The same principle is true of each individual human being, whose membership in the organic unity of the human race is as real and as essential to his very nature as man as is the eye's membership in the human body.

God, then, has made man in this twofold capacity, both as an individual and as a member of this higher organic unity. Both these sides of human nature have to be clearly grasped if we are to understand man as he really is. And since God has made man as partaking in both these capacities, He has the right to treat him as such. The basic reason the human race is a single organic unity is that human nature is one. No matter how many individual men make up the human race, they all may go to share one and the same specific human nature, and the multiplication of individuals possessing that nature does not multiply the nature as such.

This is not the case with angels; each angel is a completely distinct nature in itself, as distinct from any other angelic nature as an angelic nature is distinct from our own human nature. There is not, and there cannot be, any such thing as two individual angels sharing one and the same specific nature. Each angelic nature is unique, and human nature, no matter how many individuals share in its possession, is as truly a *single* nature as any angelic nature is.

From man at the lowest rung of rational creation to the highest angel, there is a vast ascending series of natures, each one reflecting at its own degree of limitation or finity the infinite essence or being of God, like the ascending notes of a piano or the colors of the rainbow. Each of these natures is a distinct species — that is to say, a likeness or image of the divine essence, reflecting the divine essence in a more limited manner than the species above it and more fully than the species below it; and the human species is as truly one as any angelic species. It is because human nature takes its place in the great "rainbow" or "keyboard" of creation as a single species, with its own specific "color" or "pitch," that the human race must be organically a single unit.

The reason why, on the one hand, there can be many individual men sharing one specific nature, whereas no two angels can share the same nature, would take us too deep into the region of philosophy. Suffice it to say that it is matter that makes it possible for there to be many individuals sharing one and the same specific nature, and matter is an essential element in man's nature, whereas an angel is a pure spirit, wholly free of all matter. We owe this principle to the giant mind of St. Thomas Aquinas, and it is now the accepted heritage of Catholic theology.

It is because human nature is specifically one, and the human race a single species, that it has sprung from a single origin. Adam was the source or fountainhead from which the entire human race has come forth.

We may compare him to the first cell of the human body at its conception. From that original cell the entire human body comes forth, but until that first cell commences to develop, the future human body in its entirety, made up as it is of millions of cells differentiated according to the organs they form, is potentially in that first cell; that is to say, the original cell has within it the power to produce the whole body that issues forth from it. If that cell were to die before giving rise to any further development, *the whole body* destined to come forth from it would die in it. Apply this by analogy, and we shall understand how Adam was the source or fountainhead of the single organic body of the human race, which, before it came forth from him, was still potentially *in* him.

Now, God, in creating Adam, also raised him to the supernatural state of grace. But in doing this He raised him, not merely as an individual, but as the source, as the original "cell" of the entire human race. He therefore raised the whole future race to the supernatural state *in* him. By raising this original "cell" up to the supernatural state, He gave to it the power to produce a supernaturalized body. This meant that if Adam had not himself fallen from the state of grace, every individual man who was descended from him would have been conceived in the supernatural state of grace from the first moment of his existence, an immaculate conception in every case, precisely because *the whole race as such* had been raised to the supernatural.

What, then, was the effect of Adam's fall from the supernatural state when he sinned? From start to finish, Adam fulfills the role of source and fountainhead of the race. When he fell from grace, therefore, he fell, not just as an individual man, but as the original "cell" of the whole race which as yet was still potentially in him. The whole race was still in Adam when he fell; therefore, the entire race as such fell from the supernatural state. Adam sinned as the source of the race; he fell as its fountainhead. His sin, therefore, and his fall from grace was the sin and the fall of the single organic body of the race *as such*. God had made man as an integral part of this organic unity; therefore, He treated him as such, not only when He raised Adam to the supernatural, but when Adam fell from it.

⁂

Man is born in a state of sin

Henceforth Adam's descendants were conceived and born, not in the state of grace as they would have been, but in a state known as Original Sin. It was not their own personal sin as individuals, but a state of sin belonging to the race as such. What is meant by a state of sin? It is the state of being deprived of supernatural grace while remaining destined by God for the supernatural state.

It is not the same as the state of pure nature. God could have created man in his purely natural state without ever raising him to the supernatural. In that case, the absence of grace would have been no defect in man. But God did not in fact create man in the state of pure nature, and when man fell from the supernatural, he fell, not into the state of pure nature, but into a state that is essentially a defective state, because he still remained a creature whom God had destined for the supernatural state, yet he was deprived of it.

There is all the difference between the absence of understanding in a brute animal and in a man suffering from the loss of his reason. In both cases, the power to understand is absent, but in the latter case, it is the absence of something that should be present, whereas in the case of the brute animal, this is not so. So also when man fell, the supernatural gift of grace was still something that he should have possessed because of the destiny God had planned for him; that is why his state is called a state of sin. And it is called Original Sin, because it was due to the original and primordial sin of him from whom the entire race came forth.

Is there any injustice involved by God thus allowing individual men to share as members in the fall of Adam? If God had the right to create men at all as members of a higher unity, obviously there can be no injustice, because the very fact of His creating man in this way meant that, if the head of that organic unity fell, the whole organism must fall, too. And which of us is going to presume to dictate to God? But the difficulty some people have in understanding the doctrine of Original Sin is due to their looking at only half of the question; both halves of the subject must be considered together.

For if God has permitted us individual men to share in the fall of the human race as such, He has also redeemed us, not as individuals merely, but as members of this same race. If we shared in the fall of the race, so we share in the redemption of the race as such. On Calvary, He redeemed the entire race, so that every individual member of the race, by the fact of being born into it, from the time of Adam until the end of the world, has been given the right to receive this grace of redemption. If God has treated us as members of a higher organic unity in one case, He has done so also in the other, and by the grace of redemption, He has not merely restored what we previously lost in the First Adam, but has given us back something far better in the Second Adam, our Redeemer. To ask whether God could have let us fall as members of this organic unity without also redeeming us as members is an idle question, since He has in fact not left us in our fallen condition. And we may safely say that, whatever He could have done, His goodness is such that He never would have done so.

Before the Fall, Adam was fountainhead of the human race, both in the natural and in the supernatural order. By redemption, we still have Adam as our head in the natural order; that is to say, we still draw our bodies by descent from him.

But in the supernatural order, he is no longer our head. Our new fountainhead in the supernatural order is the

Second Adam, Jesus Christ, from whom all the grace of redemption flows through the human race, backward, as it were, to Adam, and forward to the end of time. Christ our Redeemer has raised up the fallen race, incorporating it into Himself as His Mystical Body, the new supernatural organism whose members receive their supernatural life, not now simultaneously with their natural birth as children of the First Adam, but by the new birth of Baptism, whether this be the actual sacrament or Baptism of desire: "For I, if I be lifted up, will draw all things to myself."[5]

By redemption, God restored sanctifying grace to man, since without this man could never have reached the supernatural end for which God had destined him. Yet even when grace itself had been restored, there still remained the wound in man's nature that sin had inflicted, the effect of the sin and not the sin itself. The grace of redemption destroys the sin, but it does not destroy the effect of that sin in our nature, and this wound God did not remove. Although our nature has been restored to the supernatural state, it remains a wounded nature. This wound will last until the end of time; only when we receive back our bodies in Heaven will it have been healed, those spiritual

[5] John 12:32.

and glorified bodies that are to our present mortal bodies as golden wheat in full bloom is to its grain.[6]

As we shall see, God left this wound for a very good reason, but it is from this wound that arise the sufferings of mankind. Thus are the sufferings of our race due eventually to that Original Sin committed by its head. As some disease that has infected the original cell of the human body may permeate every organ and cell of the body as it grows forth from that cell, so has the poison resulting from Adam's sin, with all the suffering that results from it, passed into every member of the human race. As the sin of Adam was something that belonged to the race as such, so is suffering, the effect of this sin, our common heritage.

❦

Death is an effect of sin

In what does this wound in man's nature consist? First, there is the death of man's body. "By one man, sin entered into this world," says St. Paul, "and by sin, death."[7] Had Adam not sinned, man would have known no bodily

---

[6] 1 Cor. 15:37.

[7] Rom. 5:12.

death. All men, as each one's period of trial on earth came to an end, would have passed, soul and body, straight into the eternal vision of God, much as our Lord ascended bodily into Heaven. The death of man's body is the effect of Adam's sin.

We have a natural fear of death; we shrink from it, because it is a violence and a rending asunder of our complex nature, separating this body, which we have in common with the animal creation, from the spiritual soul, which we have in common with the hierarchy of pure spirits. Yet death is natural to the human body, as it is natural to all mere animals. The soul, on the other hand, is by nature immortal, since, being immaterial, it cannot corrupt into parts.

But as man was before the Fall, the soul had such perfect domination over the body that it communicated to it a share in its own immortality, which, while natural to the soul, was preternatural to the body. But this perfect subjection of man's body to his soul was made by God to be dependent upon man's subjection to Him as the Supreme Being. When, therefore, man refused the subjection he owed to God, his body lost its perfect subjection to the soul and thus fell back to its natural state of mortality.

Why Does God Permit Evil?

Man's senses and emotions
are no longer subject to his will

Another effect of man's refusing obedience to God was that his lower faculties, the senses and emotions, refused their full obedience to the higher spiritual faculties of his soul, his understanding and free will. "But I see another law in my members," says St. Paul, "fighting against the law of my mind and captivating me in the law of sin that is in my members."[8] There exists an internal rebellion in man, his lower nature rising up against his higher nature, a reflection within man himself of his own primordial rebellion against God.

Our Lord showed just anger when He cast the money-changers out of the Temple, but in Him there was no sin, either original or personal, and that anger arose under complete control of His will and only subsequently to His willing it. Likewise in Gethsemane, He deliberately willed to permit fear to take hold of His emotional framework. He felt crushed under it; He felt it as no other man has ever felt its awful horror, but only because He willed to allow it to take hold of Him.

[8] Rom. 7:23.

We, on the contrary, are constantly being taken by surprise; our emotions of anger, fear, lust, and all the rest rise up spontaneously before we are aware of them, and previous to the will's command. Unless checked when they first arise, they may run away with us, carrying us off our feet in a veritable storm of feeling, and grow too strong for our will to control, until they die down exhausted by reason of their own activity. Man has forfeited the complete harmony of his nature, because he himself had rejected the supernatural harmony of his own soul with God.

Since this disorder permeates man's nature throughout, and since both the sexes are part of the one nature, the wound inevitably involved a certain disharmony between the two sexes, and the external sign of this disharmony is shame. There is no way of explaining this shame that has descended upon every member of the race save by some primordial wound inflicted in man's nature.

All the faculties of man have been weakened by this lack of harmony in his nature. His intellect is subject to ignorance and error; his will no longer possesses its perfection of command and is, moreover, infected with an inherent obstinacy; his senses are abnormally drawn toward material things, impeding the intellect and will from attending to the things of God; and finally, his body is subject to diseases of all kinds. From this disorder in man arises suffering in all its forms, both mental and bodily; while from the rebellion of his lower nature against reason arises the threefold lust for sensual pleasure, wealth, and power. The lust for pleasure is manifest the world over, with its impurity, its selfish luxury, and its superficiality.

From this lust in our nature arise all the social evils of the world, bitter and narrowminded hatred between nations, and wars with all their horrors and brutality. It is the ugly wound in our nature, the poison with which the Original Sin of Adam has infected us, and which is increasingly aggravated and intensified by our own personal sins as individuals, while the activity of Lucifer, who brought about man's fall in the first instance, and of his fallen angels, still exercises itself upon man by intensifying the disorder in his passions arising from his concupiscence. Wars between nations are not only the outcome of the internal disorder in man's being, but a reflection of that conflict between the powers of good and evil in the spirit world.

۞

The earth is no longer subject to man
As man forfeited full dominion over his own self, both mind and body, so also he forfeited his complete lordship

even over the earth, so that henceforth it would yield its fruits only at the price of sweat: "with labor and toil shalt thou eat thereof all the days of thy life";[9] and the animal kingdom was likewise withdrawn from his full dominion. Scripture makes it clear that animals were fully subject to man before his Fall,[10] but "for his disobedience to God," says St. Thomas, "man was punished by the disobedience of those creatures which should be subject to him."[11] We catch a glimpse of what that original subjection of animals to unfallen man was like in its partial restoration in the lives of a few saints such as St. Francis of Assisi.[12]

Yet we should note that there are some at least apparent evils in nature that are not due to Adam's sin. What, for instance, of storms, of droughts and floods, of volcanic eruptions, and of earthquakes? In all these, there seems to be a want of balance in the distribution of energies, unnatural concentrations of it, and sudden outbursts to relieve the pent-up pressure.

[9] Gen. 3:17.

[10] Gen. 2:19.

[11] *Summa Theologica*, I, Q. 96, art. 1.

[12] St. Francis of Assisi (1182-1226), founder of the Franciscan Order.

Why Does God Permit Evil?

What, too, of animal suffering? Apart from the cruelty that man inflicts on domestic animals, do animals suffer in their wild state? Undoubtedly they suffer far less than we often suppose, since they have no power of reflection, and it is precisely man's power of reflection that so enormously intensifies his pain. Reflection enters into man's every conscious act; it is never absent.

By *reflection,* we mean this: in every act of consciousness, two perfectly distinct faculties of the mind come into play: there is our understanding or intellect, which is a purely spiritual or immaterial faculty, and there is our sense faculty producing the sense images of vision, sound, touch, and so on, and emotional feeling. These two faculties, although quite distinct, never act independently of each other; they cooperate in closest union. Whenever, therefore, any disorder takes place in our senses, whether this be an emotion, such as fear at some object of danger, or mere feeling, such as an injury received in some part of our body, our understanding is always there to "see" that disorder. In animals, this is not so, since they possess no understanding.

It is difficult for us to picture the animal mind, confined as it is entirely to sense experience, but perhaps the nearest approach we can make to it in our own experience is that level of our subconscious states which borders nearest upon the conscious.

For instance, we may be reading a book while taking our meal. If the book interests us very much, it will absorb our whole conscious attention; we are eating as we read it, yet we are not aware of this until we suddenly wake up to the fact that our plate is empty. There must have been sense imagery in our mind of the food we were eating, for unless we had seen the food on the plate, we would not have put it to our mouth, and as soon as none is left, we are aware of it. Yet we were not conscious of it, or scarcely so. Clearly, therefore, there can be sense imagery in the mind, sight, touch, taste, and so on, without consciousness in the true sense of the word. How is this possible? It is because the understanding was not "looking at" or reflecting upon this imagery, being wholly taken up with the reading of the book. Here, on the contrary, was sense imagery, the sight of the printed words, together with reflection by the understanding, and hence consciousness in its full human sense.

Since animals, therefore, possess sense imagery wholly devoid of understanding, their consciousness would seem to be something on the level of our highest grade of subconsciousness, and consequently both their pleasures and their pains on the level of our subconscious pleasures and pains experienced when our attention is taken up elsewhere.

Moreover, man's possession of understanding often leads him to associate past sufferings with that of the present in a single vision, and to foresee those that may happen in the future. Not only are animals altogether free of the higher mental sufferings experienced by man, but their very bodily sufferings seem to be of an altogether different order and on a wholly lower plane than our own. Vaguely we imagine animals to be as ourselves, and the problem is greatly reduced when we realize this.

꒜

Some evils are the effects of angelic sin

Nevertheless both Scripture and paleontology place it beyond doubt that carnivorous animals, with all their savagery and cunning, existed before man. As St. Thomas says,[13] although they were obedient to man before his Fall, they already preyed upon each other before man existed. Venomous insects and snakes, the scorpion, the boa constrictor, the octopus with its dreadful tentacles — these, like the subterranean rumblings of an earthquake, the

---

[13] *Summa Theologica*, I, Q. 96, art. 1.

blackened clouds gathering for the storm burst, and the tornado appear dark and sinister. Let us, then, not forgot that, before man existed, there occurred the first and the greatest of all sins, that of Lucifer, considered by St. Thomas to have been the highest spirit in all creation, and also of those lower spirits who joined him in revolt.[14]

It is a general principle throughout creation that a higher being can, within certain limits, act upon natures lower than itself. Plants act on the mineral matter they absorb, and animals act on the plants they eat. So, too, spirits have the power to act both on spirits lower than themselves, and also on material nature. St. Gregory says, "In this visible world, nothing takes place without the agency of the invisible creature,"[15] and St. Thomas tells us, "As the inferior angels . . . are ruled by the superior, so are all material things ruled by the angels."[16] Now, this natural power possessed by spirits over matter is common both to those who were faithful to God when put under trial and to those who rebelled, and God did not deprive

---

[14] For the nature of their trial, see Dom Anscar Vonier, O.S.B., *The Human Soul*, "Angelic Sin" (Herder, 1925).

[15] St. Gregory (d. 604; Pope from 590, writer, and Doctor), *Dialogues*, IV, ch. 6.

[16] *Summa Theologica*, I, Q. 90, art. 1.

those who fell from the supernatural state of grace of their *natural* powers. It would therefore seem that when Lucifer exercised his angelic activity upon Eve and, through her, obtained the fall of Adam, he was only doing to a rational being what he had all along been doing to inanimate nature and animal life as it developed through the ages, and this activity, coming from a spirit actuated by intense malice toward God and all His creatures, must have been such as to produce the impress of evil in a world of otherwise wondrous order and beauty. Thus do we see all physical evil to be the effect ultimately of sin, angelic or human. "All evil," says St. Augustine,[17] "is either sin or the penalty of sin."

Animal suffering, even though it be of a lower order from human suffering, cannot be, as a current opinion proposed by the late Fr. Joseph Rickaby, S.J. maintains, the inevitable outcome of the inherent limitation of created being. It is perfectly true that throughout creation, both inanimate and living, the increase of certain beings spells the limitation or extinction of others. For instance, in the mineral world, the generation of water involves the corruption of the hydrogen and oxygen that produced it,

[17] St. Augustine (354-430), Bishop of Hippo.

and reversely, the production of these two elements from water means that the water no longer exists. The speed energy of the bullet ceases when it is replaced by the heat of its impact, and every energy suffers the limitation or extinction of its own existence when it gives rise to a new energy.

The same is true of living creatures, whether in the vegetable or animal order of being. The increase of one species, or of certain individuals within a species, spells the death of others. Universally throughout creation, the good of one limits the good of another. Throughout material nature, there is a competition for existence and a survival of the fittest. This much is certain.

But the opinion referred to would have it that this limitation of created beings arising from their mutual reaction upon each other, when it applies to the animal world or at least to that higher portion of it in which feeling begins to exist, necessarily produces suffering, that the suffering of animals is the inevitable outcome of their inherent limitation as created beings, so that suffering is a necessary element in creation. But God would then be its author. Were it necessary to hold such an opinion, one might well complain that if suffering is the necessary impress of God's creative action, and since we can only know

Why Does God Permit Evil?

what God is like by what He does, then He is not that infinitely wise and powerful Being He must be if He is God at all, which is the same as saying there is no God. If, as this opinion would have it, it is intrinsically impossible for God to produce the good He has produced by creation except by means of evil, then either He is not omnipotent (in which case He is not God), or evil becomes an essential element in good, which is a contradiction in terms and is therefore itself intrinsically impossible. God is infinite substantial goodness, wisdom, and power, and it is as intrinsically impossible for the effect of His creative action to involve evil (since evil is the absence of a perfection that *should* be present)[18] as for a circle to be square.

But happily no such opinion as this is justified by facts.

Suffering and pain of any kind is, of its very nature, the signal that something has gone wrong. Consider any individual organism such as the human body. Each of its organs, heart, brain, eye, ear, stomach, muscles, and so on, is limited by the other organs. Were any of these the only organ, it would have to perform all the functions of life, whereas in fact each organ is limited to its own particular function by the fact that there are other organs to perform

[18] *Summa Theologica*, I, Q. 48, arts. 3, 5.

the other functions of the body. So long as this mutual limitation remains normal, no suffering ensues; just the reverse. Mutual limitation in this case makes for harmony and the efficiency of the whole. It is only when one of the organs *fails* in its function that suffering appears.

The same is true of nature as a whole. Where there is suffering, something has gone wrong; it cannot follow merely upon the mutual limitation of the different parts that go to make up the universe even when these are endowed with feeling. The reason is this: limitation is a mere negation, whereas any physical evil or disorder, of which suffering is the sure signal, is not a mere negation, but a privation, a failure, a defect.

A negation is the absence of some perfection in the case when that perfection is in no way owing to the thing in question, such, for instance, as sightlessness in a stone; whereas a privation or defect is the absence of some perfection that should be present, such as blindness in an animal. In both cases, there is absence of vision, but in the case of the stone, there is no reason for vision to be present and its absence is the mere limitation or negation in that stone of this further perfection; there is nothing lacking that should be there, as when vision is lacking in the animal. Now, all physical evil, which alone can give rise to suffering, is a privation, not a mere negation; it is the absence of some perfection that should be present; it is the sure sign, not of merely limited order, but of disorder.

As the animal world is now constituted, the mutual limitation of one creature by another in the animal sphere, the struggle for existence and the survival of the fittest, does seemingly involve some amount of suffering, but it need not have been so. For death is natural to all animal life, since all material things of their very nature have a beginning and an end to their existence. Death in an animal is not an evil at all, and there is nothing in animal death as such that necessarily involves suffering. Even as things are now, it seems that animals which die a nonviolent death suffer nothing. They have an instinct to retire from sight to die, but, being limited to mere sense knowledge and having no understanding (since they possess no intellect, this being a purely spiritual faculty possessed only by angels and man), they can form to themselves no concept of death or any foresight thereof. The instinct to retire from sight as death approaches is probably no more than a vaguely felt impulse to do so. Death seems to be for them no more than a gradual loss of consciousness. Animal death as such is a limitation, a negation of further life, but not a physical evil, since it is not the deprivation of any perfection that is demanded by animal nature; nor need it involve a trace of suffering, and were nature today as it would have been had it come forth untampered with from God's creative hand, there is no reason why the mutual limitation exercised by animals upon each other, involving as this would have done the survival of some and the speedier death (a nonviolent one) of others, should have involved even the first degree of suffering.

It is true we find it impossible to *imagine* the animal world as it would have been totally free of any physical evil or suffering, but this is only because our imaginative faculty is incapable of picturing anything of which it has never had actual experience. Let us consider an example: the spectrum of visible light rays constitutes merely a single octave of a large series of electromagnetic rays ranging from those of wireless telegraphy, with wavelengths of 1,000,000 centimeters, to the gamma rays of radioactivity with wavelengths of .000,000,0001 centimeter, and beyond these to the cosmic radiation, with a far shorter wavelength still. God could have provided man with a visual organ capable of reacting to all these wavelengths instead of confining him to the single octave that ranges merely from a wavelength of .00008 centimeter (red) to that of .00004 centimeter (violet), and even as it is, there is a photographic plate that reacts to the infrared heat rays so that people can be photographed in the dark. In this case, we would have been familiar with many color sensations of which, as things are, we have in fact no experience whatever and, having never experienced them, are wholly incapable of imagining them. So neither can we imagine the animal world in which there was mutual limitation and the survival of the fittest, but in which no suffering or violence was present. But this is because we have no experience of it, not because it is impossible.

One cannot escape the dictum of St. Augustine: "All evil is either sin or the penalty of sin." Suffering, and the disorders in nature of which it is the sign and the effect, is a real evil — that is to say, the privation or defect and not merely the negation of good. But since suffering is not itself sin, it must ultimately be the effect of sin. Yet animal suffering existed long before man, so it cannot be the effect of human sin. One alternative alone seems to be left: that it is the effect ultimately of angelic sin.

᪾

Man is head of the material universe
We have already expressed this opinion in outline. We may now examine a little more carefully how this could

come about. St. Augustine and St. Gregory of Nyssa both held the principle that all species of plants and animals, including the body of man, existed virtually or potentially in the primordial matter of the universe — that is to say, that the matter of the universe as it came forth in its simplest form from the creative hand of God possessed the active power to produce all these particular forms of matter; that God, in creating matter, placed in it this active power to bring forth all the different species of material beings that would eventually receive actual existence. These active powers of primordial matter St. Augustine calls *rationes seminales*, and St. Gregory (in Greek) *spermatic potencies*. Both compare the development of the universe as it is today from its primordial matter to that of a tree or plant from its seed under the influence of the active formative principle within the seed.

St. Gregory, in further comparing it to the unfolding of the human embryo, asserts that this cosmic development followed "a certain natural succession." He says, "After inanimate matter was made as a foundation, the notion of life appeared first in the form of vegetative life in plants, and then is introduced the origin of beings governed by sensation. And, according to the same order of succession . . . the sensitive may exist alone even without the intellectual nature [i.e., brute animals], but, on the other hand, the rational could originate in a body only by being mingled together with the sensitive — man was formed last of all, after the plants and animals, nature proceeding successively in a certain course toward the perfect . . . seeing the most complete perfection realized in the beings formed last of all, because of a certain necessary succession of order. For, in the rational [man] the others are also comprised, and in the sensitive the vegetative kind is also wholly included. . . . That is why nature is elevated by degrees as it were, that is through the varieties of life, from the lower stages up to the perfect."[19]

Speaking of the body of man, St. Gregory says, "Seeing, then, that the sentient life could not possibly exist apart from the matter which is the subject of it, and the intellectual life could not exist in a body except as planted in the sentient, on this account the creation of man is narrated as coming last, as of one who *took up into himself* every single form of life, both that of plants and that which is seen in brutes. His nourishment and growth he

---

[19] *De opificio hominis*, ch. 8; cf. E. C. Messenger, Ph.D., *Evolution and Theology* (Burns, Oates, and Washbourne, 1931), 133-134, from which these quotations are taken.

derives from vegetable life. . . . His sentient organization he derives from the brutes. But thought and reason is incommunicable, and is a peculiar gift in our nature to be considered by itself."[20]

By this last sentence St. Gregory marks the clear distinction between man's spiritual soul, created directly by God, and his body, formed from matter by the inherent powers placed in matter at creation, for man stands midway between the angelic hierarchy of pure spirits and the material universe. He has an intellect and a will, purely spiritual and immaterial faculties, in common with the angels, and he has a body in common with the animals. All material creation leads up to man (and to any other rational animals that may exist elsewhere in the universe) as its culminating point, and for the formation and support of whose body it has been created, a body so perfect as to become the partner of his purely spiritual soul, by which man becomes not only the head of the material universe, but the lowest rung in the angelic hierarchy.

There is, then, throughout the evolution of the material universe, from its earliest nebulous beginnings, a definite

[20] *De Anima et Resurrection;* cf. Messenger, *Evolution and Theology,* 135.

succession, each grade coming into being only after the formation of the lower grade immediately preceding it, as its proximate origin makes this possible. This is so in a growing embryo: the optic nerve cannot develop before the brain, being an outgrowth from it; for the same reason, the brain must follow the medullary canal, and this the primitive ectoderm. And St. Gregory realized very clearly the analogy between the embryo and the universe as a whole. But this natural succession in the development of nature has no meaning save as the working out of some definite plan in the mind of God, and the end of the plan is man himself.

꙳

God works through created things

How, then, was the execution of this plan ensured? A multitude of active agencies will not cooperate harmoniously toward producing a certain effect according to a previously devised plan unless they are guided and directed in their action. Left to themselves, they will produce any kind of chaos; only a directing mind can bring together many things toward a single, common end. Ultimately, of course, this mind is the divine mind, but here we are faced with a principle on which St. Thomas insisted most strongly, and which is in practice admitted at least implicitly by all men in everyday life: that, except in the case of miracles, God works through created things as His instruments.

Whenever we look for the cause of anything that has happened, it is for the natural or created cause that we look, not to God's direct intervention, although we realize that the created causes themselves have no existence or power of action save from God. St. Thomas says the more power God has given to created causes to produce their own effects, the more does it manifest the perfection of His own creative act, and "to detract from the creature's perfection is to detract from the perfection of the divine power."[21]

Abbot Vonier, commenting on this principle of St. Thomas, says, "It is a part of Protestant mentality to feel worried and annoyed at what is called 'the being that stands between man and God.' . . . But this objection, if carried to its logical extent, would make nature itself not only superfluous, but burdensome. . . . The Protestant mind mistakes exclusiveness for immediateness; it thinks that man is near to God because there is nothing but God. The Catholic view, on the contrary, is that the greatest

[21] *Contra Gentiles*, Vol. 3, ch. 69.

and highest communication of God is communication of causality. . . . The direct and immediate executive powers of Providence are the celestial spirits; they are Providence in practice, and therefore they become one of the main factors in the world's course. We can never give too great prominence to the Scholastic principle that God never does through Himself what may be achieved through created causality. It would be quite within the spirit of Catholic theology to say that for any result which does not require actually infinite power, God will sooner create a new spiritual being capable of producing that result than produce it Himself."[22]

♰

Angelic sin is responsible for
some of the disorder in the world

Now, the evolution of the material universe leads up to man as its end, and to man raised to the supernatural state. It is therefore all included as part of God's providence over man. St. Thomas, in teaching that God administers His providence through angelic agency, says, "All things that operate do so as instruments moved by

---

[22] Anscar Vonier, *The Human Soul*, 3rd ed., ch. 48.

Him, and serve Him obediently, so as *to bring forth into the world the order of providence which He has planned* as from eternity."[23]

Taking this principle of St. Thomas concerning angelic agency in the execution of providence, together with the principle of St. Augustine and St. Gregory concerning the active powers of primordial matter, both principles operating with man as the end toward which they lead, we are brought face-to-face with what is a very majestic vision of God's working in the universe — namely, that He has at the beginning of creation infused into the highest angels the knowledge of His plan for the material universe. This plan has been passed down the vast angelic hierarchy, by what St. Thomas calls "angelic illumination,"[24] from those highest spirits, whose sublime natures are exclusively concerned with the contemplation of God, to those lower spirits, to whom is committed the guardianship of man and the exercise of activity on material things, much as by analogy the general plan of campaign in the mind of the commander-in-chief is passed down and distributed among the various grades of subordinate military

[23] *Contra Gentiles*, Vol. 3, chs. 78-80, 94.

[24] *Summa Theologica*, I, Q. 106; cf. *The Human Soul*, ch. 51.

authority, until it reaches the sergeants and privates, each of whom knows no more than his own particular part of the job, and who puts his part into actual execution.

These lower spirits, by operating on the active powers of matter, do not supplant their activity, but stimulate their action, as, for instance, gunpowder explodes by its own inherent force, yet it cannot do so without a fuse; the fuse does not supplant it, but sets it into action. Thus, by their united cooperation upon the forces of primordial matter through the long ages, angelic agencies have set them into action according to the definite plan of God, drawing out this plan by successive stages rising upward through the electronic, mineral, vegetative, and sentient spheres.

We may summarize this grand picture with a homely analogy. In the making of a pudding, the various material agents, fire, milk, eggs, flour, and the rest, produce the finished article by their own inherent activity; the cook himself adds no material forces to them whatever. Yet these material agents would never produce the pudding without the cook, in whose mind is the plan or recipe of the particular kind of pudding to be made, according to which he brings the various agencies together in such order and proportion as only a cook knows how.

Now, St. Thomas tells us that "the Devil was one of the angelic powers who presided over the terrestrial order,"[25] and it is a commonplace in pagan countries that numbers of inferior fallen spirits also exercise power over the human race. Even had man not fallen, he would still have needed guardian angels as protection against these apostate spirits and the physical evils in nature.[26] God did not withdraw their natural powers over matter when they fell from grace; indeed it seems that this directive power over material creation is so much part of their very natures that only by annihilating them could God have caused it to cease, and God never "undoes" creation.

A cook, intent through some malicious motive on spoiling his master's dish, could introduce certain of the ingredients in wrong proportions. For instance, a certain proportion of salt or pepper often improves a dish, but if introduced in excess will produce a very different effect as certain culinary accidents may have led us to experience. The cook is still using the same ingredients; but it is the proportion in which they are introduced that is at fault.

[25] *Summa Theologica*, I, Q. 110, art. 1.
[26] Ibid., Q. 113, art. 4.

Why Does God Permit Evil?

So the fallen angels who have power over the universe, and of this planet in particular, being motivated by an intense angelic hatred of God and of all creatures, have acted upon the forces of matter, actuating them in false proportions so far as lay in their power, and this from the very outset of evolution, thus producing a deep-set disorder in the very heart of the universe, which manifests itself today in the various physical evils we find in nature, and among them the violence, the savagery, and the suffering of animal life. This does not mean that, for instance, an earthquake or a thunderstorm is due directly to satanic action. It is due to purely natural causes, but these causes are what they now are because of the deep-set disorder in the heart of nature resulting from this action of fallen spirits, most subtly mingled with the action of good spirits, throughout the long ages of the world's formation: "An enemy came and sowed tares also amid the wheat."[27]

Were there nothing more in nature than the limitation of one creature by the more successful growth and activity of another, we would expect to find among animals that the less successful would die, as indeed the majority probably die now, by a nonviolent death involving

[27] Matt. 13:25.

no pain, the mere negation of further life. But in actual fact, the animal world is heavily armed with weapons of slaughter that have anticipated those of man's invention. It is a reign of violence and savagery that is an enigma to many who forget that the fall of the angels is a tremendous reality, but which is well understood if it be the reflection in the material and sentient sphere of that spirit savagery and violence of apostate angels who have set themselves in a state of intense hatred against God and all that He has created, and who, being unable to hurt God Himself, seek to satisfy their hatred of Him by marring the beauty of His creation to the utmost of their power. We find implicit recognition of this when St. Peter speaks of the Devil as "a roaring lion going about seeking whom he may devour."[28]

If this work of evil spirits has intermingled with that of good spirits throughout the ages from the beginning, both working simultaneously, although with that of the good spirits altogether predominating, we need not be surprised at their subtle blending. Among the lowest animalcules in which no consciousness can exist, one may say that when, for instance, millions are swallowed at a time by a passing

[28] 1 Pet. 5:8.

whale, there is nothing more than the negation or limitation of further existence. But as animal life rises imperceptibly through its first stages of dawning consciousness, this limitation exercised by one creature on another takes on, again almost imperceptibly, the coloring of violence in some form. Among higher animals, this subtle intermingling is more apparent. Is not the eagle most beautiful in the very act of circling over its prey? Indeed we find the same thing among the inventions of man; is not the bomber a most beautiful thing because perfectly adapted to the function of flight? Yet it presents a sinister appearance owing to the destructive end for which it is built. One may be drinking in the beauty of a summer day, when suddenly a rabbit screams across one's path pursued by a stoat. One's sense of the rightness of all natural things is disturbed, and one feels one is not the victim of mere sentiment; yet the stoat, with all its vicious cruelty, is a lovely animal.

The natural foundation of animal life is the vegetable grade of being. While plants feed directly upon mineral matter, they themselves provide food for the animal grade immediately above them; and there seems to be no reason to suppose that there would have been any departure from this rule in the direction of carnivorous feeding had there been no extraneous influence for evil from still higher, namely, angelic grades of being, any more than man would have turned to artificial clothing in place of his natural covering now lost, except for the entry of sin into the human race. If we class animalcules too low in the scale for consciousness together with vegetable life as the natural food of animals, we may suppose that the higher animals would not have been impelled to seek elsewhere for sustenance by means of attack upon creatures sufficiently developed to feel. In this case, the lower animal life, as soon as it rose in the course of evolution to that grade of sentient structure which permitted of consciousness, would simultaneously have been provided with means of maintaining its independence from being an object of food, and this without the danger of attack from others; while, of course, other types would have been evolved than those that now constitute the carnivorous species.

With regard to physical evil in nature, therefore, we are faced with two alternatives: either it is not really evil at all but only apparently so, and in that case, animal suffering is also merely apparent; or else it really is physical evil, in which case, it must ultimately be, with animal suffering included, the effect of some sin that preceded man, that is to say, of angelic sin. But sin is precisely the one thing that comes entirely from the rational creature and in no way whatever from God. All else whatsoever that the creature has is from God, but sin, being a privation or defect, is wholly the creature's own doing. The sufferings of animals, therefore, if they are real, are in no way the effect of God's creative act.

There is no more difficulty in understanding that God should permit animals to suffer as the effect (indirectly) of the action of evil spirits than in understanding the established fact that He permits them to suffer from human cruelty. Yet there remains this difficulty with regard to animal suffering that does not present itself in the case of human suffering — namely, that animals, since they have no spiritual souls and are therefore incapable of a future life, can receive no reward for their sufferings.

To this we would reply with two preliminary considerations that, while not fully solving the difficulty, do much to minimize it. In the first place, as we have already pointed out, their suffering is of an altogether lower order than our own, owing to their possessing no more than sense imagery with no intellect to "see" their own sense suffering, still less to foresee it; just as they are incapable of the joys and happiness of man as a rational and immortal being, so correspondingly they are incapable of his suffering; the degrees of each are correlative.

In the second place, their pain is greatly outweighed by well-being and pleasure, so that they are better off than if they had not existed at all, yet none of us raise as an objection to the divine goodness the fact that an innumerable multitude of merely possible animals will always remain as mere possibles and never become actually existing. But the real reason God permits them to suffer even though they are incapable of a reward seems to be that, while God has made angels and men directly for Himself, He has not made animals directly for Himself, but for man, and as dependent both upon him and upon the spirit creation of which man forms the bottom rung. Animals, therefore, have been made wholly dependent upon those for whose sake they exist, and dependent, therefore, on their behavior for good or ill.

St. Thomas tells us that the material universe and the spirit hierarchy do not constitute two universes, but one. When, therefore, these intellective beings (angels and men) fell by sin, the nonrational universe, as made dependent on them, fell with them. St. Paul says, "For we know that every creature groaneth and travaileth in pain even till now."[29] Nonrational creation, animals included,

---

[29] Rom. 8:22.

has no existence save for the sake of rational creation; therefore, God has permitted it in its own way to share in the fall of the rational creature who has sinned. And granting this as the reason for God's permission of their suffering, it still remains a suffering altogether lower in kind than our own, and when death ends their existence, the balance of their lives has been altogether on the side of pleasure and the well-being of life, and a greater good than if they had not existed at all."[30]

※

God brings good out of evil

But to return to human suffering: Is it contrary to God's goodness that He should permit sin, and hence its effect, suffering? If God were constrained by His goodness to prevent sin, it would follow that, since an act of sin is a free act of the will, He would either be prevented from creating beings with free will at all, or be constrained to

[30] It is particularly interesting to find the same explanation of animal suffering given by one who, although not a Catholic, has come independently to the same view: cf. C. S. Lewis, *The Problem of Pain* (The Centenary Press, 1940), 121-124. See also M. C. D'Arcy, *The Pain of this World and the Providence of God* (Longmans, 1935), 75-80.

treat them as though they were not free. In either case, He would be limited by the malice of His own creatures and so be dependent on them. That cannot be.

Moreover, the role of providence is to preserve, not to destroy, created natures. It would be contrary to divine wisdom to create free will and to prevent its execution, and against divine goodness to disrespect the dignity of free will, pretending it to be other than it is. There is no pretense about providence. Man, as the result of his sin, is fallen and wounded, and God has treated him as such. He did not pretend the Fall had never taken place and merely remove its effects. He did much more. He treated man for what he really was, and from his Fall raised him to a state higher than would have been his had he not fallen. Was not the final state of the prodigal better than the first pre-cisely because he had fallen? St. Thomas says, "For God allows evils to happen in order to bring a greater good therefrom; hence it is written: *Where sin abounded, grace did more abound* (Rom. 5:20). Hence, too, in the blessing of the paschal candle we say, 'O happy fault, that merited such and so great a Redeemer!' "[31] Again, in St. Augustine's words, "God judged it better to bring good out of evil,

[31] *Summa Theologica*, III, Q. 1, art. 3.

than to suffer no evil to exist";[32] or, to use Fr. Martindale's happy phrase, "God can not only sterilize old sins, but transubstantiate them into good." To transubstantiate evil into a still greater good, there lies the genius of the supernatural!

We may perhaps be allowed an analogy, not an elegant one, but to the point. It is that of a manure heap. The lady of leisure will have nothing at all to do with it. This is ultimately how the natural man regards suffering. But for the peasant, it is something most precious. He does not avoid it, but uses it. He carts it, spreads and ploughs it in, and thence draws crops that are his life and sustenance. It is the same thing in both cases, but differently dealt with. While the natural man seeks escape from suffering by any means, provided only that his "honor" be maintained, the supernatural man, while taking what natural remedies God provides, is always ready for it. He does not seek to escape it, but to use it, and God says of the soul well manured with suffering what Isaac said when blessing Jacob: "Behold the smell of my son is as the smell of a plentiful field which the Lord hath blessed."[33]

[32] *Enchiridion*, ch. 27, t. 3.

[33] Gen. 27:27.

The Church, in her Liturgy on Holy Saturday, actually falls into an ecstasy of joy, not only over suffering, but even over the very sin that caused it, not, of course, on its own account, but because of the good that God has drawn from it: "O truly necessary sin of Adam which has been blotted out by the death of Christ! O *felix culpa!* O happy fault that has won for us so loving, so mighty a Redeemer!" How different is this from Nirvana, escape from conscious existence, from the stern aloofness of the Stoic, from the mean sheltering under the Epicurean's carefully selected program of pleasure from the cruel defiance of Nietzsche! The Church's note, contrasted with these like midday brilliance to the blackness of night, is joy, for she has found the pearl of great price hidden within the shell of evil. We must, then, consider these strong words of her Liturgy, for in them is contained the answer to a riddle that, without grace, the human mind has ever failed to solve.

*

God has brought about
great good from man's Fall

Dame Julian of Norwich, one of our English mystics, during the series of visions granted her in May 1373, heard our Lord say, "It behooved there should be sin, but all shall be well, and all shall be well, and all manner of thing shall be well."[34] She then asked, "Ah! good Lord, how might all be well, for the great hurt that is come by sin to Thy creatures?" Our Lord replied, "Adam's sin was the most harm that ever was done, or ever shall be, to the world's end, [but] this amends-making [redemption] is more pleasing to God and more worshipful, without comparison, than

[34] Bl. Julian of Norwich (d. c. 1423), *Revelations of Divine Love*, ch. 27; that is, it behooved that God should permit sin as man's deliberate choice, thus respecting the freedom of his will even when he abused its power.

ever was the sin of Adam harmful"; moreover "since I have made well the most harm, then it is my will that thou know thereby that I shall make well all that is less."

※

God grants man a greater
good than he lost in the Fall

St. Paul had said the same: "But not as the offense was the act of grace. For if by reason of the offense of the one, the many died, much more have the grace of God and the gift . . . been lavished upon the many. . . . But where sin hath been multiplied, grace hath abounded yet more."[35]

The Fathers repeat this; thus, St. Leo the Great: "For when the entire human race had fallen in its first parents, God in His mercy willed in such manner to bring succor, through His only-begotten Son, Jesus Christ, to the creature made in His own image, that its second state should excel beyond the dignity of its original state. Happy if it had not fallen from what God made it, but happier if it remain in what He has remade."[36]

---

[35] Rom. 5:15, 20.

[36] St. Leo the Great (d. 461; Pope from 440-461 and Doctor), *Sermon 72*, ch. 2.

Yet no words can compete with those of the Liturgy itself. Listen again to its jubilant song: "O truly necessary sin of Adam which has been blotted out by the death of Christ! O *felix culpa!* O happy fault that has won for us so loving, so mighty a Redeemer!"

Let us, then, consider how God has drawn from Adam's fall a good still greater than that which he had lost.

Since the encyclical *Eterni Patris* of Leo XIII, the Church has continually insisted on the teaching of St. Thomas Aquinas. In her Code of Canon Law, she gives authority to his doctrine in a manner which is entirely unique.[37] Pius X said, "To follow Aquinas is the safest way to a profound knowledge of divine things,"[38] and Pius XI, "His doctrine the Church has made her own. . . . To all who hunger for truth we would say, *Go to Thomas* for the food of sound doctrine."[39] Although this in no way binds us to hold the view of St. Thomas in every particular case, as Pius XI makes quite clear, yet with such sanction we may safely follow him when he says that, had man not fallen, the Eternal Word would not have become

[37] Canon 1366.

[38] *Motu proprio*, 1914.

[39] *Studiorum Ducem*.

incarnate."[40] As usual, he is endorsing Catholic tradition. St. Irenaeus says, "For if flesh had not needed to be saved, in no wise would the Word of God have become flesh";[41] St. Athanasius: "The Word would by no means have been made man, unless the need of man had been the cause thereof";[42] and St. Augustine: "If man had not perished, the Son of Man would not have come. . . . There was no other cause of the Lord Jesus Christ coming in the flesh, except to save those who before were in the death of their sins."[43] Scripture names man's salvation alone as the reason for God's becoming man; and it seems that the words of the Liturgy, when it speaks of Adam's "necessary sin"[44] and "happy fault," would be meaningless were it otherwise. The character of the Incarnation is intrinsically one

[40] *Summa Theologica*, III, Q. 1, art. 3.

[41] St. Irenaeus (c. 125-c. 203; student of St. Polycarp, missionary, Bishop of Lyons, and Church Father), *Adversus haereses*, Bk. 5, ch. 14, no. 1.

[42] St. Athanasius (c. 297-373; Bishop of Alexandria and Doctor), *Oratio 2 contra Arianos*, no. 56.

[43] *Sermo 174*, ch. 2; *De peccatorum meritis et remissione*, Bk. 1, ch. 26, no. 39.

[44] Necessary, not because God *could* not, but because He *would* not, have become incarnate unless man had fallen.

of mercy. Had man not fallen, God would indeed have loved him as He loves the angels, but He would not strictly have shown him mercy. The Incarnation has the character of a mother's pity for her child who has tumbled and hurt himself. She loved him before, but never so much as she does now. The caresses she now lavishes upon him would have been mere extravagance before; now they are the spontaneous overflowing of a heart whose floodgates have been opened.

The parable of the Prodigal Son may be taken as our Lord's description of the Redemption. The elder son, his churlishness apart, represents man's elder brethren the angels. The prodigal is the human race. Had he not fallen, there would have been no festal robe, no ring, no merry feast with fatted calf. Unfallen man, like the angels, would have possessed the supernatural state of grace and would have been destined for the vision of God; and since grace is a partaking in the divine life itself, one might have thought this was the closest union possible between a creature and God. Yet what of redeemed man? By the Redemption, God has raised mankind again to the supernatural state, but in a more wonderful way than before he fell.

Our Redeemer is Jesus Christ, who is God incarnate, and in Him there are two distinct natures, the divine and the human, yet only one Person, that of the Eternal Word, the second Person of the Blessed Trinity. Therefore, when He performed any human act, it was nevertheless the Person of the Word who acted. It was the Word who suffered, who spoke with human lips, who played with toys and handled the chisel.

But God's plan of redemption is that we men should be united with Jesus Christ the Incarnate Word by a union so close that St. Paul can find no analogy to express it except the union between the different members of the human body and their head as a single living organism. This union of each one of us with Christ (and so indirectly with each other) is the closest possible union that even God could devise, for we are "incorporated" into Christ[45] as living members of His Mystical Body, forming with Him one supernatural organism. This union is a supernatural one, but since the supernatural order is higher than the natural order and in every way more perfect, the union between

---

[45] "At no time," says St. Thomas, "not even before the coming of Christ, could men be saved unless they became members of Christ [*Summa Theologica*, III, Q. 68, art. 1; Acts 4:12]. . . . But before Christ's coming, men were incorporated in Christ by faith in His future coming," and by even implicit faith (*Summa Theologica*, III, Q. 69, art. 4; II-II, Q. 2, art. 7 and Q. 1, art. 7).

Christ and us is closer and more real, not less so, than the union between head and members in the human body. As Leo XIII says, "The eternal Son of God wished to assume human nature in order to redeem it. To do this, He had to consummate a mystic union with the entire human race."[46]

Without the Fall, our head would have been a mere man, the First Adam; by redemption from the Fall, our Head is the Incarnate Word, the Second Adam: "For as *in Adam* all die, so *in Christ* all shall be made to live."[47] Our Lord Himself has said, "I am the Vine, you the branches"[48] (and how could He express a closer union than this, for between a vine and its branches there is identity). And St. Paul, while using the analogy of the human body instead of the vine, teaches us the same thing: "For as the body is one and hath many members, and all the members of the body, many as they are, form one body, so also it is with Christ. . . . Now you are [together] the body of Christ, and severally His members."[49]

---

[46] Encyclical *Octobri mense.*

[47] 1 Cor. 15:22 (Westminster Version).

[48] John 15:5.

[49] 1 Cor. 12:12, 27.

Why Does God Permit Evil?

As head and members of the human body are united into a single organism by the soul, which is its principle of unity and which is wholly present in every cell of the body, so are we united with the Incarnate Word as a single mystical organism by the Holy Spirit, who dwells both in the humanity of Christ the Incarnate Word and in each of us, and who was sent down by Christ on the day of Pentecost to weld us into this organic unity; so that St. Thomas says we constitute with the Incarnate Word "one mystical Person,"[50] or, to use St. Augustine's words, "the whole Christ." Each of us is a cell in Christ's own Mystical Body. By the grace of redemption, man has been drawn to a union with the Person of the Eternal Word that is second only to the Hypostatic Union of Christ's own sacred humanity with the Word, so that not only the individual Christ, but "the whole Christ" is drawn up into the Blessed Trinity, at the right hand of the Father, as a single God-Man, one body and one person.

Such is the gesture of God's mercy toward fallen man. It is the Father's welcome to His prodigal come home. Instead of restoring man to what he had been, God has bent down from His eternity, taking him into His arms and

---

[50] *Summa Theologica*, III, Q. 19, art. 4.

pressing him to His heart in an embrace so close that the gulf between Creator and creature has been bridged, God and man henceforth forming in the order of grace a single being, "the whole Christ." This wondrous embrace, which eternity itself will not unlock, has not been granted to the angels.

Henceforth humanity, by its nature lower than the least of angelic natures, has, by its incorporation in Christ, been raised above all creation. Already by nature man is high priest of the material universe, since in him its mineral, living, and sentient perfections are gathered up and given the voice of rational praise. But by the Redemption, the vast angelic hierarchy itself praises God through Jesus Christ, that is to say, through our human nature, itself lower than any angelic nature.

For in the Preface of the Mass, the Church jubilantly sings, "It is truly meet and just . . . that we should always and in all places give thanks to Thee, O holy Lord, Father almighty, eternal God, *through Christ* our Lord, *through whom* the *Angels* praise Thy majesty. . . ." Humanity, which in the natural order is lower than all angelic natures, is raised by its incorporation in the Incarnate Word above the entire angelic hierarchy. Lowest by nature, it is highest by grace. As Joseph was thrown by his brethren into a pit, and was thence raised to be ruler over Egypt second only to Pharaoh, so has man been cast by his jealous elder brethren, the rebel angels, into the pit of Original Sin, and from that pit has been raised by God, as "the whole Christ," over all created being, with the Godhead alone above him.

⚜

Individual creatures experience
different degrees of glory

But if human nature as such has been raised to a dignity so far surpassing that which it would have attained without its "happy fault," to what extent is this true of particular individuals who share this nature, apart from the humanity of Jesus Christ Himself? For, although our human nature as such has been raised above all creation through its supernatural union with the Person of the Word, it does not follow that we all, as individuals, share equally in this elevation of our nature by grace.

In the first place, theologians agree that our Lady, because she is the Mother of the Incarnate Word, immeasurably exceeds by her grace, and therefore by her glory also (since glory in Heaven is the fruit of grace on earth), the glory of all angels together, and yet by nature she will ever remain lower than the angelic nature, since she is human.

Some idea of what this means may be gathered from St. Thomas's teaching concerning the hierarchy to which we have already had occasion to refer, namely, that no two angels are of the same nature.[51] As we have seen, men differ as individuals only, and all have the same human nature, whereas each angel is a distinct nature in itself, unique throughout all creation, and excels the angelic nature next below it as greatly as the lowest angel excels man. God's purpose in creating was to manifest His own infinite glory, that there might be created beings who should share His own infinite bliss, and who should themselves reflect in a finite manner, as far as this is possible, His own infinite Being.

We have said that the angelic hierarchy may be likened to a rainbow. In the rainbow, the colorless light of the sun, which we may take to represent the single infinite perfection of God's Being, which contains virtually and in an eminent manner the multiplicity of all finite perfections, is split up into a number of distinct colors: violet, indigo, blue, green, yellow, orange, and red. Each

[51] *Summa Theologica*, I, Q. 1, art. 4.

color is a partial reflection only of the colorless light, and each color differs in nature from the rest, for each has its own specific wavelength. Violet has the shortest wavelength and therefore the highest energy; red has the lowest energy. So the angelic hierarchy is a vast rainbow, reflecting the infinite Being of God in as many finite ways as there are angelic natures, each angel possessing its own specific spirit energy, and no two angels being alike any more than two colors are alike. As violet differs from green or red, so one angel differs from another. As the lowest angel vastly excels our human nature, so the next angel in the hierarchy vastly excels the lowest angel, and so on upward throughout the whole angelic hierarchy — and this not merely in degree, as one man excels another, but by possessing an altogether higher nature, more powerful and more beautiful.

On the other hand, by this same analogy of color, men differ from each other, not as a number of different colors but as a number of objects which are all of one and the same color, all, for instance, red, since men do not possess each a distinct nature, but differ merely as individuals all of whom share the same human nature.

The next thing that St. Thomas tells us is that the number of angelic natures is "far beyond all material multitude."[52] We need not examine what exactly this means. It will suffice merely to think of the number of grains of sand on any stretch of seashore, or of drops of water in the ocean, and then to remember that the whole earth is but a small planet among myriads of stars far larger than the sun, to enable us to realize that if the number of angels is far beyond all material multitude, their number is beyond all reckoning. No multitude of finite things can be actually infinite, so let us (for lack of a better word) call their number quasi-infinite. This word seems the only one to use if we are to convey what St. Thomas has in mind — namely, that the reason for the immeasurable vastness of their number is that nothing less could in any way adequately reflect God's glory, which is infinite.

Abbot Vonier says, "Angels are innumerable. The number of angelic spirits has always been considered as one of the marvels of God's power that baffle the mind of man."[53] The angelic hierarchy, then, is an unimaginably vast rainbow reflecting in a created manner the uncreated glory of God, a quasi-infinite series of ascending natures, each unique in creation, each higher than the next, with

[52] *Summa Theologica*, 1, Q. 1, art. 3.

[53] *The Human Soul*, "The Numbers of the Angels."

humanity at the foot of this hierarchy, for man is set "a little lower than the angels."[54]

Finally, St. Thomas explains that the supernatural glory of each angel is proportionate to his nature.[55] The higher his nature, the higher is his glory. What, then, must be the glory of the highest angel in creation? Obviously in view of these facts, it is so stupendous as wholly to exceed our power to grasp.

Had Adam not fallen, man, like the angels, would have received grace and glory proportionate to his nature. And since his nature is the lowest in the angelic hierarchy, it follows that no member whatever of the human race would have been as high in Heaven as even the lowest angel. Yet Mary, although she is lower by nature than the lowest angel, is immeasurably above the highest angel of this immense hierarchy by reason of her glory. She is Queen of Angels. If, then, the glory of the highest angel is so tremendous, what must Mary's glory be? It leaves the mind completely dazed.

Mary's glory is indeed unique, because she is the Mother of God Incarnate. But it is Catholic tradition that the rest

[54] Heb. 2:7.

[55] *Summa Theologica*, I, Q. 62, art. 6.

of the human race will share in varying degrees in this elevation of our nature by grace, so that the human race will not form merely the lowest rank in the angelic hierarchy in Heaven, as it would have done had man not fallen, and the great saints at least will be raised in glory even into the highest angelic ranks.

"The elect of the human race," says Abbot Vonier, "are believed to be assumed into the very hierarchy of the angels, into the ranks of the Cherubim and Seraphim and all the other orders; the elect of the human race will not be only the outside fringe of the spirit world; they will, on the contrary, be shining stars in every one of the spirit planes."[56] Thus, in the Vesper hymn for the feast of the Passing of St. Benedict (March 21) we find these lines: "And now in the bliss of Heaven he rejoices 'mid the burning throng of Seraphim."

Upon this same principle, moreover, there is every reason to suppose that great multitudes of the human race, apart from the great saints, will be raised in this manner into the angelic hierarchy in degrees depending on the grace offered to each one and the correspondence given

---

[56] Anscar Vonier, *The Angels* (London: Burns, Oates, and Washbourne, 1928), 86.

thereto. "This equality," says Abbot Vonier, "is entirely based on grace. Human nature will ever remain what it is, vastly inferior to the angelic nature; but such is the power of grace that the inequality of nature is bridged over, and that an elect of the human race may truly become, in all literalness of language, the equal of the highest angel, and that consequently he will be vastly superior to other angels of lower rank."

The significance of this will be grasped when we realize that the degree of our bliss in the eternal vision of God will be the greater according as we are raised higher in the angelic hierarchy, and that anything we can possibly suffer on earth is as nothing in comparison with even the smallest increase of glory in eternity. One may add that even those of us who will be lower in Heaven than any angel will still possess a peculiar dignity not shared by any angel by reason of our membership in that Mystical Body whose Head is the Incarnate Word. Such is the manner in which God has dealt with fallen man.

We have already seen how God has permitted individual men to share in the Fall of the First Adam by reason of their being members of the one race that fell in him. We have now seen the counterpart of this: how individuals are raised high in the angelic hierarchy by sharing in the elevation of the Second Adam above all creation. This would never have been so had God redeemed us as mere individuals. It is precisely because we are redeemed as members of the Mystical Body of Christ, of the one race re-elevated by Him to the supernatural, that we are enabled to share in the elevation of Christ's own humanity above all created being. We became subject to Original Sin because we fell in Adam; we are raised higher, we may say almost immeasurably higher, in Heaven than we ever would have been, because we rise in Christ.

If anyone is tempted to see a difficulty in our becoming involved in the sin of the human race as such, let him not forget God's answer to this catastrophe — namely that, precisely because of this, we have become involved also in the *felix culpa*, the Redemption of this same race, by incorporation into a Head greater beyond measure than the head that fell.

Wonderful as all this is, one feels tempted to ask whether the title *felix culpa* finds its full justification if there be many members of the human race who pass out of this world in a state of personal and mortal sin, for if that be so, it means separation from God that nothing can reprieve. Such was the question in Dame Julian's mind when she received answer from our Lord: "That which is impossible to thee is not impossible to me. I shall save my word in all things, and I shall make all things well."[57] What, indeed, do we know of that last mysterious moment, wholly hidden from the eyes of men, when the soul passes from time into eternity? That this takes place after apparent death seems certain, since the Church provides that the Sacrament of the Sick still be administered conditionally after all signs of life have ceased. It is God's secret, but this we know: that "His tender mercies are over all His works,"[58] and that, "by showing mercy, He most perfectly manifests His omnipotence."[59]

At death each soul comes face-to-face with Infinite Mercy, to accept or to refuse irrevocably. Yet we know that some souls will be lost.[60] It is therefore good to remember that it is not God who damns a soul; it is the soul that damns itself by its final and irrevocable rejection of God, so that even God's omnipotence *cannot* change it without destroying its free will, and that He will never do. The will's choice, once made with full and exhaustive vision of

[57] *Revelations*, ch. 32.

[58] Ps. 144:9 (RSV = Ps. 145:9).

[59] Collect for the tenth Sunday after Pentecost.

[60] Matt. 25:41.

the entire issue, is by its very nature irrevocable, since there exists no new motive that can ever be offered to change its decision already made. It is set like steel for God or against Him. Such was the choice of the angels at their trial; such is our own at death.

For the will never changes its decision except in response to some new motive offered by the understanding, but at the trial of the angels, and at that of the human soul at its departure from the body, God so enlightens it that *all* the motives whatsoever are seen in a single glance. No new motives therefore remain that can occasion any new decision on the part of the will. Having made its decision in the full light of all the motives that could possibly draw it, this decision of its very nature cannot be anything else than final.

If we hold a blackened glass before our eyes, it will change the effect of the sun's rays upon us, yet the sun itself remains unchanged. Now, God is ever changeless as the sun — an eternal fire of infinite love, pouring forth grace with ceaseless activity. It is the sinner who changes the *effect* of that love upon himself from mercy into justice.

It is the steel-hard malice of the created will, whether angelic or human, that makes Hell, not God.

Why Does God Permit Evil?

In the Liturgy, man offers infinite praise to God

From all that we have said so far, it is clear to what extent the answer to the problem of evil in human life centers on the tremendous fact of Christ's Mystical Body. We may now turn to consider the Liturgy, for the Liturgy is the prayer of Christ's Mystical Body as such. Since we are both individuals and members of this Body, we possess this twofold capacity where prayer is concerned. Our prayer as individuals is our private prayer, as well as those devotions made in public that nevertheless are not recognized by the Church as her official public prayer. The Liturgy is the Church's public and official prayer, consisting of the Holy Sacrifice of the Mass in the first place, and of all the sacraments, and of the Divine Office. It is our prayer as members of Christ's Mystical Body, because it is the prayer of Christ Himself uttered by the lips of His Mystical Body. Every human act of Christ, since it was an act of His divine Person, had an infinite value.

But we are Christ's own members, and just as the movement of one's hand is not an isolated act of that member, but an act of the human person to whom that hand belongs — it is *I* who write *with* my hand — so in the supernatural order of grace, our acts as *members of*

Christ are acts of His divine Person, for, as St. Thomas says, we constitute "one mystical Person" with Him. From eternity and before creation, the Word has offered to the Father a hymn of infinite praise. When Christ praised His Father with human lips, it was still this same praise uttered by the Person of the Word, brought from Heaven to earth, from eternity into time when the Word became incarnate. But we are the lips of Christ, His members through whom He offers His eternal praise.

"This," says Abbot Marmion, "is the Liturgy. . . . It is the praise of Christ, the Incarnate Word, passing through the lips of the Church. She sings the canticle sung *in sinu Patris* by the Word, and brought by Him to earth."[61] The united praise of all the angels through eternity has but a finite value, yet man is the mouthpiece of praise that is infinite.

Yet it is in the Holy Sacrifice, the central act of the Liturgy, that this identity between Christ and His members is most closely drawn. On Calvary, the Man Christ, by reason of His divine Person, offered a Sacrifice of strictly infinite value. But from the Council of Trent we know that the Mass is the same identical Sacrifice, save for the

[61] Columba Marmion, *Christ the Ideal of the Monk*, ch. 13.

manner of offering. In the Mass, the priestly offering of Christ and of celebrant are identified. The priest says, "This is *my* Body . . . *my* Blood." Moreover, every Catholic also truly offers this Sacrifice: "Pray, brethren, that *your* sacrifice and mine may be acceptable . . ."; for the Mass is the Sacrifice of "the whole Christ," of both Head and members.

The praise of the entire angelic hierarchy, tremendous as it is, is no more than finite, yet man, "set a little lower than the angels," offers a sacrifice of strictly infinite praise and of infinite expiation for sin. He offers in one Mass more than all angels, without the Mass, can offer through eternity. They indeed praise God through the Mass, yet the Mass is not strictly their sacrifice. It is man's sacrifice, since its Priest and Victim is man, not an angel. In the Mass, God has given to man something immeasurably surpassing anything he would have possessed had Adam not fallen, for the Mass is the greatest thing, not only that is, but that ever could be outside the Godhead. And since the Mass has its consummation in Heaven, its infinite praise, offered by man to God, will never cease through all eternity.

Throughout God's dealings with fallen man, one thing stands out most markedly: it is what we may call God's matchless courtesy. He never patronizes man as a philanthropist. God could have said to man, "You have made a mess of things, so I will put it right for you." But He was honoring man far more highly when He said, "Since you have made a mess of things, I will help you to put things right yourself." Man had sinned; therefore, it was to be man, the Second Adam, who should pay the price of sin and regain God's friendship.

Man had freely submitted to Satan, and Satan had thereby gained over man a stolen sovereignty, the first and cruellest of all tyrannies. Satan, once the highest spirit in creation (if we follow St. Thomas), had browbeaten and seduced the lowest rational being in creation; therefore, Satan should himself be defeated and cast out by One bearing our own human nature so vastly lower than his own, a humiliation on which his cruel pride will have eternity to meditate.

There is, as we have seen, something infinite about the guilt of sin, because, although man, who commits it, is a mere finite creature, yet the majesty and sanctity of God, against whom it is committed, is infinite. For this reason, man was, by his own power, wholly incapable of expiating sin, since no honor, no sacrifice, no expiatory act he could offer to God could exceed a finite value. By the

Why Does God Permit Evil?

Incarnation, God has placed it in man's own hands to offer to God an act of expiation of strictly infinite value. Thus it comes about that God has drawn from the infinite evil of human sin the strictly infinite good of His Redemption, by which man himself, although a mere finite creature, will offer to God through eternity praise that infinitely exceeds the sum total of praise offered by the entire angelic hierarchy.

No need, then, to "excuse" God apologetically for permitting evil! However great be the ocean of human suffering on earth, even so in view of the principle of the *felix culpa,* a concrete fact with eternal consequences beyond our present power to conceive, evil's enigma vanishes as a candle flicker in the blazing sunlight of God's omnipotent love. It is difficult for us to *feel* this now, because so long as we remain on earth, our sufferings loom large, while the reality of the next world is often scarcely felt. But it is not the office of faith to impress the feelings, even though it sometimes flows over into them in moments of great joy; faith is a supernatural light in the understanding by which we assent to the truth of its teaching and act upon it, and that is what matters.

This principle of the *felix culpa,* moreover, permeates the entire redemptive dispensation. As God has dealt with Adam's sin, so will He deal with our own personal sins, "transubstantiating" them into good, if we leave Him free to act in us by our humility and our childlike confidence — "for since I have made well the *most* harm . . . I shall make well all that is *less*."

Epicurus said, "Omnipotence could, Benevolence would have prevented evil." "Omnipotence could," oh, yes! But "Benevolence would"? Epicurus could not see through the canvas. Only from above, by supernatural light, can we see the divine needlework. Omnipotence could, but, ever reverencing man's power of free choice, divine love would not prevent evil, for the sheer joy of pouring forth such an abundance of mercy, of stooping to embrace man in the Incarnation, and of raising him to such a height. Man is God's fallen child, God's darling, overwhelmed with torrents of divine mercy. O *felix culpa!* The Church speaks no hyperbole, just the plain truth.

✲

The good use of
suffering brings a reward

Yet this deep mystery of the *felix culpa* has still to be completed, for God has chosen suffering, the effect of sin, as means whereby to bring about this work of sin's destruction. Sin has become the victim of its own offspring. Suffering has been raised to a supreme height of honor in the Church, because Christ chose it before all else as the means of redemption. His smallest act, being infinite, could have paid the debt of justice, but it could not satisfy the generosity of love. God cannot but hate suffering as such, since it is evil. No father takes pleasure in his son's wounds received in battle, yet he will not prevent them because he knows that they are necessary if heroic love will have its way. In this way God permitted suffering, in this way the Man Christ accepted it, since by no other means could redeeming love find its full expression. It was love that chose it.

Now, the Church is Christ's own Mystical Body so that her life is Christ's own life growing through time to full maturity. Her life must, therefore, necessarily conform to His.

⚜

Christ's life was, in a sense, a failure

First, then, what of Christ's own life? We need not mince matters. His life was in one respect, and truly, a failure. He endeavored to teach His chosen people that He had come to set up a kingdom that, although on earth, was yet a spiritual and not a temporal one. Had He succeeded, we cannot say what would have happened. We may surmise that He would have established His worldwide spiritual authority in Jerusalem, the holy city of His chosen people, and have ascended to Heaven without crucifixion or death, delegating, as now, that authority to Peter and his successors. In fact, He was rejected, and the sin of Jerusalem wrought her own destruction under Titus.

Christ failed to teach the peasantry of Galilee because they were so gross. They could understand only such a king as would free them from the Roman yoke. He failed to teach the Pharisees because of their malice. There were indeed times when He seemed on the verge of success. On Palm Sunday, all Jerusalem went out to meet Him delirious with joy. His very enemies had perforce to admit "the whole world is gone after Him."[62] Then, within a week followed collapse, inexplicable and complete. The hopes of all were shattered. Only His Mother understood.

It was failure, and let us write it in large letters. Failure, yes, but He could have prevented it, had He willed. "No man taketh my life away from me, but I lay it down of myself."[63] But He would not force man. Omnipotence allowed Himself to fail, but once granting this, He really did fail, and the culmination of His failure was Calvary. He permitted failure. In what? In that which concerned the *visible* success of His spiritual kingdom *on earth*. Never did He permit the least failure to impede His one essential purpose, the redemption of the human race. Nay more, it was precisely from His failure, namely, His Passion, that He drew forth that redemption whose power is infinite.

Next, what of the Church's life? The Church is continuously subject to forces that work for failure in her visible life on earth. There is relaxation and betrayal from

[62] John 12:19.
[63] John 10:18.

within and, often as the result of these, persecution from without. The Church, too, seems so often on the verge of some great success, then all is swept away. The history of her monasticism is one of alternate vigor and decay. Her enterprises succeed up to a point and no more. The premature finish to St. Francis Xavier's[64] mission to the East, the tragic end of the Jesuit Reductions in Paraguay, that "Christian Indian state" as they have been called, leave one dazed.

In the thirteenth century, Catholic principles were permeating an entire civilization, and then, just as success appeared, germs of decay set in. Worldly principles worked their way into the fabric of society, and immorality into the very papal court. In reaction came the bitter zeal of Luther and others who, had they been humble, would have been reformers instead of destroyers.

True reform came with the Council of Trent, but by then whole countries had been lost to the Faith, and anti-Christian ideals led step by step to excessive industrialism and a materialistic philosophy, and so by reaction have produced Marxism and the anti-God campaign.

[64] St. Francis Xavier (1506-1552), Jesuit missionary to the East Indies.

The good use of suffering brings a reward

Today we see what remains of our Christian civilization seriously threatened, on the one hand by atheistic internationalism, and on the other by exaggerated nationalism with its international jealousies and blind hatreds, the disastrous effect of rejecting that Catholic Faith which alone can weld all the peoples of the earth into a harmonious unity. Christendom has been broken up. Palm Sunday and Good Friday have been lived again.

Picture the world today if the Church had full rein, with her millions united around the Holy Sacrifice and fed daily upon the Bread of Life; with her religious institutes for teaching, for nursing, for the poor and the penitents, for every need of humanity. Think of society based upon the principles of social justice as set forth in papal encyclicals. Recall her monastic and liturgical life when all her energy was free to develop it. Or again, consider her architecture and crafts, her "by-products," as we may call them, when her own spirit and not that of commercialism permeated society, so that a trained sense of beauty was the common heritage of a civilization and not the painful experience of a few.

Yet, in contrast to all this, we have seen Catholic schools swept away to make place for those of neopaganism, and children from their tenderest years "educated" amid all the horrors of Soviet schools. The Church's visible success on earth seldom, if ever, attains its full development, and at times is swept away. For Christ did not promise a heaven on earth, but in eternity. His kingdom is *in* this world, but is militant and not *of* the world.

What, then, of the Church's one essential end, the incorporation of all men in Christ? Evil is flashy, boisterous, and proclaims itself aloud. Grace is silent and works deeply. Throughout the seeming chaos, grace does its work, serene and all-powerful. Let us never forget that on Calvary Satan was cast out; he still lashes with his tail, but with the fury of despair. Christ is complete Master of the world; in ruling it, He is omnipotent: "All power is given to me in Heaven and on earth."[65] He could prevent all evil whatsoever. In actual fact, He in large measure permits it, but only because His power can draw from it still greater good.

༈

We are often blind to God's work in the world
Could we but see below the surface of the world's history, we would understand, for grace is a work within the

[65] Matt. 28:18.

souls of men mostly hidden from our eyes, yet universal and almighty. The malice of the human will can oppose Him, but only to break itself upon this Rock, changing the omnipotence of mercy into the omnipotence of justice. His ways are hidden now, awaiting the Judgment when all will be revealed.

"There be deeds evil done in our sight," writes Dame Julian, "and so great harms taken, that it seemeth to us that it were impossible that ever it should come to good end. . . . And the cause of this is that the use of our reason is now so blind, so low, and so simple that we cannot know that high, marvelous wisdom, the might and the goodness of the blissful Trinity. And thus meaneth He when He saith, 'Thou shalt see thyself that all manner of thing shall be well.' "[66]

The evil conditions among which so many souls are set appear to our human eyes indeed as well-nigh beyond hope. "The English public," wrote Francis Thompson, "with all its compassion for our destitute children, scarcely realizes . . . that they are brought up in sin from their cradles, that they know evil before they know good, that the boys are ruffians and profligates, the girls harlots, in the mother's womb." Yet so great is God's power and wisdom

[66] *Revelations*, ch. 32.

that He can make use even of the worst conditions for His own ends in such manner as surpasses the understanding of our weak intellects.

We are like bats, which can see only by faint light; the full light blinds us. God measures His graces to the conditions of each soul, and His works are always perfect. Through every event in the lives of men throughout the world, Christ's power pours out upon the human race, permeating every crevice as brilliant sunshine on a summer day.

⚹

Christ still suffers in His Church

As it was by His Passion that Christ effected the salvation of the world, so it is by her passion that the Church continues it. The Church "fills up" those sufferings that are still lacking to "the whole Christ." The Church will go on suffering until the world's end, but with the passion of victory, for her passion is the extension of Christ's Passion and therefore an extension of His redemptive victory: "*Rejoice* when men shall persecute you unjustly for my name's sake."[67] As Christ taught with authority, so does the Church; like Him, she does all she can; then — but

[67] Cf. Matt. 5:11-12.

only then — when she fails, she rejoices, for she knows that all her suffering, united with the redemptive Sacrifice of the Mass, is still greater even than all her other works for souls.

If such be the meaning of those sufferings that affect the Church as a whole, what are we to think of the sufferings of individuals? Is not the world borne down under their weight? We have only to reflect for a moment to realize how universal suffering is in the world, and so much of it that is not due to the fault of the individual who has to bear it. Of the man who was born blind the disciples asked our Lord, "Who hath sinned, this man or his parents, that he should be born blind?" And Jesus answered, "Neither hath this man sinned, nor his parents."[68] Widespread poverty is more often caused by the avarice of a successful few than by the sloth of the poor; injustice brings ruin to those who are guiltless of it themselves; plague and famine sweep away thousands of innocent victims. The list is endless, and there is no need to pursue it further.

All suffering is due eventually to sin, but not necessarily to the sin of the individual who suffers, nor even to his immediate forebears. It is due to our solidarity as members

[68] John 9:2-3.

of the human race, which, as a single organic whole, fell in Adam, its head, that we as individuals share in the sufferings of the whole. For, as we have said, when Adam sinned, he sinned not merely as an individual, but as head of this organic whole, so that, just as in the case of the human body, if the head is shot, the entire body dies and not merely the head alone; or again, as the entire stream is poisoned if its spring and fountainhead are poisoned, and not merely the spring, so when Adam, by his sin, fell from the supernatural state of grace, the whole race as an organic unit fell in him, for as yet it had not issued forth from him. For, as we have said, God has made us, not as isolated individuals merely, but as members of this organic unit we call the human race, so that when the entire race fell as a single body in Adam, it inherited *as a single body* the suffering which resulted from that fall, and each of us bears his share of that suffering by the sole fact of being born into the race as one of its members.

But if God has allowed us to suffer by reason of our membership in that organic whole which had the First Adam as its head, so, too, He has allowed us to merit through suffering by reason of our membership in the Mystical Body, which has Christ, the Second Adam, as its Head. And by this second membership, we gain far more than we lost by the calamity of our first membership, for "where sin hath been multiplied, grace hath abounded yet more."

If we are in the state of grace, we are living members of Christ's Mystical Body, and this is no mere form of words, but a tremendous reality. Christ the Head and we the members form, in St. Thomas's words, "one, mystical Person," so that when Saul inflicted suffering on the Christians, Christ said to him, "Saul, Saul, why persecutest thou *me?*"[69] Our membership in Christ is not just a beautiful idea, but a concrete fact with practical consequences. As head and members of the human body live by one and the same lifeblood, so do we live by the supernatural life of grace that flows to us from Christ, our Head. Christ has willed in this way to identify each one of us with Himself, for He has said, "As long as you did it to one of these my least brethren, you did it to *me*."[70]

⚹

Christ has sanctified suffering

Therefore, when we suffer, it is Christ who suffers in us, His members. Christ can no longer suffer in His natural

[69] Acts 9:4.
[70] Matt. 25:40.

body since He is in Heaven, but He can suffer in us, the members of His Mystical Body, and precisely because we are His members, all suffering that takes place in us draws its supernatural value from the suffering He endured in His Passion. On Calvary, Christ used suffering as the instrument by which He won for us the grace of redemption. By doing this, He has sanctified human suffering for all time and has given to all our suffering a quasi-sacramental value. That is to say, whenever He permits any suffering whatever, be it great or small, to come to any of us, that suffering comes to us as a channel of grace. As it was by His own suffering as Head that He merited grace for us, so by our sufferings as members He transmits grace to us.

Suffering, therefore, holds a central place in the scheme of Redemption by reason of the part it played on Calvary. Being itself the effect and penalty of sin, Christ has, as it were, seized hold of it and used it as the instrument of His act of redemption, so that henceforth suffering and grace are, as it were, knit together. Not that our sufferings are the principal channel through which grace flows from Christ to us, for this principal channel is the sevenfold channel of the sacraments. Yet suffering, which we may call a quasi-sacrament, never comes to us save as a channel of grace. We may rebel against it; then we block the flow of grace into us and render the suffering fruitless. Or we may accept the suffering as the will of God for us (that is to say, accept it with our will, for the senses may rebel involuntarily in spite of our good will); then inevitably grace flows into our souls and increases the degree of sanctifying grace that is already ours and hence, if we persevere to the end, increases the degree of our future glory in Heaven, which is the fruit of grace. And since we never merit further grace for ourselves without in some measure meriting it also for others, since we are "members one of another" in the Mystical Body of Christ, it follows that our willing acceptance of suffering has its supernatural effect in our fellow members throughout the world, so that we share by participation in Christ's own redemptive work for the salvation of mankind.

By our willing acceptance of suffering, therefore, Christ continues to suffer in us, and to work out to its completion through the centuries the effect of His redemptive act for the salvation of the human race performed once for all on Calvary. This is the meaning of that supernatural joy in the presence of suffering that is characteristic of saints.

"What is the instinct," writes Msgr. Hugh Benson, "that makes the Carmelite hang an empty cross in her cell, to remind herself that she must take the place of the absent figure upon it — and yet keeps the Carmelite the most radiantly happy of all women? The joy of a woman . . . over her first child is but a shadow of the solemn joy of a Carmelite, the irrepressible gaiety of a Poor Clare — women, that is, who have sacrificed every single thing that the world thinks worth having. The thing is simply inexplicable except on one hypothesis: that that unique thirst of Jesus upon the Cross is communicated to His members, that His ambition to suffer is perpetuated continually in that Mystical Body in which He re-enacts the history of His Passion. . . ."[71]

The world, too, is full of those faced with well-nigh impossible conditions heroically borne, and in some measure a good use of suffering must be the vocation of us all. The Carmelite and others like her have sacrificed everything, but at the same time, they are free of many responsibilities and anxieties that it is the necessity and duty of those living in the turmoil of the world to face: children to feed and educate, the home to maintain, and this maybe in face of ill-health and the constant threat of unemployment. Neither cloister nor world escapes suffering, which

[71] Hugh Benson, *Christ in the Church* (Longmans), 187.

is the common lot of all men, but each supports its own peculiar burden.

How, then, does God treat those whom He loves most? "Whom the Lord *loveth* He correcteth, and He scourgeth every son whom He accepteth. . . . As with sons, God dealeth with you. For where is there a son that his father doth not correct? If ye are without correction . . . ye are bastards and not sons."[72] And Christ Himself has said that "every branch that beareth fruit He cleanseth, that it may bear more fruit."[73]

We have only to think of Christ's own Mother at His birth to realize that, had we been in her place, we would have complained that God was providing *absolutely nothing*. But as we look back, we understand. It is the very fact of the extreme poverty of Christ's birth that has won the heart of the human race. God was providing, but in His own way, not ours. It is our duty to do what lies in our power to support those who have a claim of dependence on us. But if, in spite of this, God seems in our case also to be providing absolutely nothing, then let us remember Mary and Joseph at Bethlehem with their unique and

[72] Heb. 12:6-8 (Westminster Version).
[73] Cf. John 15:2.

tremendous responsibility, and we shall understand more easily why it is so with us.

Each one of us has his own sufferings often quite un-suspected by any other. Perhaps they are physical; they may be mental or spiritual, bereft of glamor, humiliating to the last degree, without seemingly any compensating feature. We think things are "going wrong," whereas in re-ality these misfortunes are the necessary condition of our progress. "You remember in the Scripture," says Fr. Bede Jarrett, O.P., "how with touching beauty He compares the way He deals with souls to the mother eagle teaching her young to fly. . . . Nearly always out of every brood there is one that grows timid, that has not the courage to flutter off the rock where the nest lies. Then the mother bird takes twig by twig the nest away from the ledge. She will make the nest most bereft, desolate, lonely. . . . Do you re-member how the prophet describes that, at last, but not impatiently, only with exquisite and disciplined affection, the mother eagle will beat the little one off the ledge with her wings. Then, as it falls, crying with terror, she dives un-der it and catches it between her wings. Then she shakes it off again, and again dives under and holds it between the spread of her wings, until at last what of itself it would not dare do, it is made to do. It finds that flying is not so difficult as it dreamt. In our life, whatever is done is done by divine action. Does this better explain your life to you?"[74]

Again, souls who are to advance along the way of prayer must be purified. Far more souls are called to simple contemplative prayer than is generally supposed, and this is true of all states of life. Not all indeed are called to the same degrees of contemplative union with God, but those whom God calls to the closest union are precisely those whom He seeks to purify most. It is because we have a fallen nature that God must purify us before such close union with Him is possible.

"The more terrible and black the darkness," writes Abbot Chapman, "the greater the purification, and the closer the union with God." In such cases, the mind may be so clouded that it can do no more than accept the suffering with the unfelt apex of the will. "You can't *feel* this," he continues, "or the trial would cease. But you can act upon it, and that is what matters. . . . Accept what God wills, even accept *not being able to feel that you accept.* But trust (without knowing that you trust) and go on."[75]

---

[74] Bede Jarrett, *No Abiding City* (London: Burns, Oates, and Washbourne), 53.

[75] *The Spiritual Letters of John Chapman*, 2nd ed. (London: Sheed and Ward, 1938), 148.

Why Does God Permit Evil?

But by far, the greater number of those who suffer have no knowledge of suffering's value. What, for instance, of the great mass of the people subjected to the unspeakable horrors of a war in which they have no say? What of the thousands of unemployed, of casual jobbers with a family to keep, or of the down-and-out? How many of these understand why God permits them to suffer this? Furthermore, what can the millions in pagan lands know of the supernatural merit of suffering, and how, therefore, can the sufferings of these be meritorious?

⚜

The Church has a visible and an invisible membership

No man's acts can be supernaturally meritorious unless he is himself already in the supernatural state of grace. We may, therefore, be allowed a digression here to explain how it is that these millions of pagans who still constitute so great a part of the world's population can have any part in the supernatural order of grace at all, seeing that they have not received the sacrament of Baptism by which man is "born again" into the supernatural state of grace as a member of Christ's Mystical Body, and that "outside the Church there is no salvation."

The good use of suffering brings a reward

In the first place, the Catholic Church, founded by Christ Himself upon the Rock of Peter, with its head and center in the Vicar of Christ, is identical with the Mystical Body of Christ; the two names are synonymous. It therefore constitutes with Him, as we have seen, "one mystical Person" and, as "the whole Christ," perpetuates His incarnate life throughout the centuries until the world's end. There can be no salvation outside the Body of the Church, precisely because it is the Mystical Body of Christ who is the sole source of grace for all men. Again, as Christ's Mystical Body, it forms with Him a single living organism and must therefore, by its very nature, be one and undivided, since no living organism can be anything else; and since an organism is essentially a visible thing, the unity of Christ's Body the Church must be a visible unity, possessing a visible body and a visible head on earth. We are incorporated into this visible Body of the Church by the sacrament of Baptism, and by the full adherence to the teaching and authority of the Church, which is the normal development of the grace of Baptism. We thereby become *visible* members of the Body of the Church.

But besides this visible membership, there is also an *invisible* membership, which, although invisible and therefore imperfect, is yet true membership of the one visible

Why Does God Permit Evil?

Body of the Church. The analogy of the human body used by St. Paul only imperfectly represents this invisible membership, although we may call the internal organs of the human body invisible in a sense. But since the perfection of Christ's Mystical Body altogether exceeds that of any merely natural body, that which is only imperfectly represented in the latter case can exist literally and perfectly in the former.

"Those who labor under invincible ignorance of our most holy religion," says Pius IX, "but who carefully observe *the natural law* [that is to say, pagans] and its commandments *written by God in the hearts of all men* [Rom. 2:13-16] . . . are able through the efficacious power of divine light and grace to attain eternal life."[76] But St. Thomas tells us that "at no time, not even before the coming of Christ, could men be saved unless they became members of Christ."[77] It follows, therefore, that such men as these are true members of Christ's Mystical Body; yet their membership is not a visible membership, since they have neither received the sacrament of Baptism nor given any visible adherence to the teaching or authority of that

[76] *Quanto conficiamur maerore*.

[77] *Summa Theologica*, III, Q. 68, art. 1.

Body. They are therefore invisible members of this same Mystical Body. Both its visible and its invisible membership, therefore, are contained under the organic unity of this one visible Body of Christ.

How, then, are they incorporated into Christ's Mystical Body as His invisible members? St. Thomas gives us the answer. It is by their implicit faith, or, which is the same thing, by their implicit desire for Baptism — that is to say, by Baptism of desire.[78]

Recent exhaustive research has established beyond all doubt the universality among all peoples, both primitive and civilized, of some belief in God and divine providence; and however much this has in many cases become contaminated with superimposed error, it is not effaced. All the evidence goes to show that pure monotheism was the religion of early man, nor is it wholly obscured in the later polytheism, even though more external attention be paid to lesser deities which for such peoples may be said to hold much the same place as the canonized saints do for Christians. It was the aim of the materialistic evolutionists to show that there existed atheistic tribes possessing no religion, since they would allow to man no spiritual

[78] Ibid., Q. 69, art. 4.

soul created by God and infused into the newly formed body at conception. For them, man was a glorified brute animal and no more. It was therefore essential that they should be able to produce some evidence. Their failure to do so after making so many statements based on observation entirely superficial and unscientific makes a sorry spectacle in face of the more recent and compelling evidence against them.

First of all, there were the godless Andamanese; then an Englishman who lived among them for eleven years showed them to have, not only a religion, but an elaborate one. Then there were the Australian Aborigines whom Huxley described as a people in whom "no cult can properly be said to exist." This gratuitous statement, which was unworthy of any man professing science, was exploded by Howitt, a distinguished ethnologist, who, unlike Huxley, had made a careful study of these natives at first hand and whose authority with regard to them has been surpassed by no one.

The Indians of Guiana were the next presented as the people who had no conception of God. The fact is that they held their religious belief so sacred that they refused to manifest it to the first stranger who came along. Long and careful study proved them to be profoundly religious and that they worshiped God under the titles of "Our Maker" and "Our Father," a title eventually sanctioned by the prayer given to mankind by our Lord Himself.[79]

Sir John Lubbock asserted the atheism of the Dalrymple Island natives, basing this statement on the authority of a Mr. Jukes who had spent one day in the islands.[80] Again, careful observation proved the falsity of this statement.

"But the search for godless tribes went on," says Archbishop Downey, "and goes on, despite the testimony of such eminent authorities as Max Muller, Ratzel, de Quatrefages, Tiele, Waitz, Garland, and Peschel, all of whom are agreed that there are no races of men without religious belief and practice"

St. Thomas says, "Although they [the Gentiles before Christ] did not believe in Him explicitly, they did nevertheless have *implicit faith* through believing in *divine providence* . . . and all the articles of Faith are contained

---

[79] Archbishop Downey, "Rationalizing the Gods," *The Clergy Review* (January 1931).

[80] *Studies in Comparative Religion* (Catholic Truth Society), Vol. 1. See also Andrew Lang, *The Making of Religion*, 3rd ed. (1909); Rev. W. Schmidt, S.V.D., *The Origin and Growth of Religions*, trans. H. J. Rose (Methuen, 1931); and Otto Karrer, *Religions of Mankind* (Sheed and Ward, 1936).

implicitly in certain primary matters of faith, such as God's existence and His providence over the salvation of man, according to Hebrews 9: "He that cometh to God must believe that He is, and is a rewarder to them that seek Him." For . . . *belief in His providence includes all those things which God dispenses in time for man's salvation. . . ."*[81]

Belief in God and His providence, then, as found among all peoples, both civilized and primitive, is *implicit faith in the full content of revelation* as found in the Catholic Church alone, and by this faith, says St. Thomas,[82] such men (even those who lived before Christ "by faith in His future coming") are incorporated into Christ, that is to say, into His Mystical Body, the Church, so "that the Body of the Church is made up of the men who have been from the beginning of the world until its end."[83]

---

[81] *Summa Theologica*, II-II, Q. 1, art. 7.

[82] Ibid., III, Q. 68, art. 1.

[83] Ibid., Q. 8, art. 3. To speak of those outside the visible unity of the Church as being "in the soul" of the Church finds no place in the theology of St. Thomas. Matter that is "in" a soul, i.e., vitalized or "informed" by it, by that very fact becomes part of the living organism belonging to that soul. Men, therefore, who are "in" the soul of the Church, i.e., supernaturally vitalized by the Holy Spirit, are thereby part of the Body of

The membership of these is an invisible membership, even though the Mystical Body of which they are members is essentially a visible body. St. Thomas, quoting St. Augustine, says, "Some have received the invisible sanctification without visible sacraments," and adds, "Since, therefore, the sacrament of Baptism pertains to the visible sanctification, it seems that a man can obtain salvation without the sacrament of Baptism, by means of the invisible sanctification"[84] — namely, by his implicit faith and implicit desire for Baptism, for such as these "receive grace and virtues through their faith in Christ and their desire for Baptism, *implicit* or explicit."[85]

Speaking again of those who are in invincible ignorance, Pius IX says, "Who would presume to assign the boundaries of such ignorance in view of the variety of nations, regions, characters, and so many other circumstances?"[86] There are some Catholics who speak as if it

the Church. The distinction to be drawn is not between those in the Body and the Soul of the Church, but between the visible and invisible members of one and the same Body.

[84] Ibid., Q. 68, art. 2.

[85] Ibid., Q. 69, art. 4.

[86] *Singulari quodam*.

were beyond question that the majority of those outside the visible unity of the Church, at least pagans, were lost. They presume, where Pius IX says, "Who would presume?" And since St. Thomas says that the sanctification of these is an invisible one, and therefore seen by God alone, by what extraordinary favor of God do they presume to see into the secrets of these men's souls? Such gratuitous expressions of opinion do great harm and would enormously restrict the Catholicism of the Church, which is universal, not only potentially with regard to her visible members, but actually with regard to her invisible members.

Commenting on 1 Timothy 2:4 — "Who will have all men to be saved and to come to the knowledge of the truth" — Père Fernand Prat, S.J., says, "The thought of the Apostle is so clear that no sophism can obscure it. . . . *God wills the salvation of all men,* which must be understood of all without exception, since no exception is indicated, but is, on the contrary, excluded by the emphatic character of the discourse and by the repetition of the word *all* four times. It is in vain to object that the divine wish to save is necessarily limited by the addition that all may come to the knowledge of the truth, for, we are assured, since this second proposition cannot be absolutely and universally true, the first one cannot be either. The reply is easy: all human beings have not the use of their reason, but all, without a single exception, are capable of eternal salvation; thus, while the phrase referring to the knowledge of the truth limits itself naturally to men who are capable of knowing it, the other phrase is limited by nothing and should, according to the rules of sound exegesis, retain its full significance."[87]

Since, therefore, Christ redeemed the entire human race as such, thereby giving to all men without any exception a claim to receive the supernatural life of grace, it follows that the *invisible* membership of Christ's Mystical Body must include all whatsoever who do not reject the grace offered them, that is to say, all men of genuine good will, according, to the angelic promise in which no restriction was named: "peace on earth to men of good will."[88]

It is in this sense that Leo XIII says that the eternal Son of God consummated "a mystic union with the entire human race," so that the Mystical Body of Christ as including its invisible membership is nothing less than the

---

[87] Fernand Prat, *The Theology of St. Paul* (London: Burns, Oates, and Washbourne, 1927), Vol. 2, 77-78.

[88] Luke 2:14.

human race itself, resupernaturalized by Christ the Second Adam, excepting only those members of the race who die in the rejection of grace, so that the unity of the Mystical Body is the unity of the human *species* itself of which we have already spoken, of the redeemed species taking its place among the supernaturalized angelic species in the great hierarchy of creation.

The unity of the Mystical Body of Christ, therefore, is as essential to its very being as a specific organism as is the unity of each angelic species. And since the Catholic Church is identical with the Mystical Body, it is not merely a society within the human race, but, as including its invisible membership, the redeemed race itself, only those being outside its invisible membership who reject the grace of redemption and prefer the society of fallen angels. But this invisible membership is membership of a Body that is itself essentially a visible Body, and it is only because of the imperfection of this membership that it does not share in the visibility of the Body to which it belongs; and to be outside the visible unity of the Catholic Church for any reason other than invincible ignorance must involve ill will, so that such a man would not be a living member of Christ's Mystical Body at all. "If, with the best will, thou art ignorant," says St. Augustine, "it will not be reckoned against thee for sin, but if thou refusest to enquire, thou art guilty."

It is not, therefore, for us to limit the invisible membership of Christ's Mystical Body, and, granting invincible ignorance, the two Pauline conditions are sufficient for salvation — namely, belief in the existence and providence of God, if acted upon. But all men, with few exceptions, believe in God and His providence over us. Many would not admit this even to themselves, yet deep down in their souls they believe, for, as St. Paul tells us, all men have the natural law of God "written in their hearts." To come to a knowledge of God is a deep instinct of man's nature, and belief in Him, however little adverted to and confused with error, is strongly rooted in the human heart. At times, moreover, and to the surprise of the man himself, it finds expression in prayer.

The writer well remembers how a young Australian soldier in 1917, who paraded the fact of having no religion, after telling of a terrible bombardment he had gone through, added, "And I don't mind telling you fellows I damned well prayed. You may not believe it, but it's a fact." Such men as these are legion, and insofar as they sometimes raise their souls Godward, they are making an act of faith in God's providence. But, to recall the words of

Why Does God Permit Evil?

St. Thomas, "Belief in His providence includes all those things which God dispenses in time for man's salvation," and therefore involves implicit faith in everything that God permits in our regard, and consequently in the true supernatural value of suffering.

This is true even of many, probably the great majority, of those who call or think themselves atheists. The Spanish bishops, in the joint letter issued during the country's civil war, declared that "the vast majority of our Communists have at the moment of death been reconciled to the God of their fathers." Professor Allison Peers relates several stories of these Spanish Communists.[89] There is that of the man who emerged from an ugly-looking crowd that was threatening a Holy Week procession in Seville: "I am a Communist and an atheist," he cried, "but, by God, if one of you lays a finger on this statue of our Lady, I'll shoot him dead." There is also the case of the Communist who said to our Lord in the tabernacle, "I had sworn to be revenged on You," then, firing his revolver at Him, said, "Surrender to the Reds! Surrender to Marxism!" Whatever else these men were, they were not atheists.

---

[89] *Spain, the Church and the Orders* (Eyre and Spottiswoode, 1939), 181, 184.

The good use of suffering brings a reward

Fifty years of persecution in Russia failed to drive out religion from the people of that country. But what shall we say of those who foster this persecution?

God alone knows how many of these men possess fundamental good will, and how many are deliberately rejecting God to gain their materialistic ends in defiance of Him. And let us Christians beware lest, by our self-complacence and neglect of God, we cause scandal to our fellowmen and imperil our own souls. Eternity is too high a stake to trifle with. We who possess the light of faith have the greater responsibility. But, putting aside those who are knowingly resisting God, one may say that, seeing our complex nature, a man who has been his own companion for half a century and more may still be a stranger to himself. Some theory of a godless universe built up in the conscious mind may be entirely walled off from a conviction born of faith hidden away in the depth of his intellect. While his will may be parched with thirst for God, so parched and dry that the senses can in no way feel it, the thirst is there, and at death, when already the senses have ceased to function and the superficial theories they encased have vanished, that thirst, springing from the roots of faith buried deep down in the soul, will insist on being slaked at the inexhaustible Fountain of living waters.

Why Does God Permit Evil?

The secret depths of this great multitude of souls are visible to God alone. But this we can say with certainty, that all those who are in good faith and yet have no more than implicit faith in God and His providence, while they make no explicit act of accepting suffering for the love of God, do implicitly accept it insofar as their souls are orientated Godward at all. Clearly their limited faith is excused only by invincible ignorance, and the merit of their act will not be so great as that of one who is explicitly accepting suffering with a full knowledge of its value. But insofar as any man, provided he is faithful to the light he possesses, implicitly accepts what providence ordains, he is in some measure meriting an increase of grace by the suffering he endures. We say "in some measure," but God's measure is always generous beyond anything we can imagine.

In the war, we saw the cheerful fortitude, not only of our fighting men, but of civilians under the grimmest bombing raids. One may say that in many cases this is merely natural virtue, but in view of St. Paul's statement that "where sin hath been multiplied, grace hath abounded yet more," the writer, for one, cannot doubt that grace is behind it, raising that natural virtue to the supernatural level, and that such cheerful fortitude is at least implicit love of God and perhaps of a very high order, and may put to shame the narrow selfishness of many a pious person who grows irritable as soon as his or her pious exercises are interrupted by the needs of others.

꙳

Children may also merit grace through suffering

But what are we to say of the sufferings of little children? The case of these is different, because in order for any act of ours to be meritorious, it is essential, in the first place, that we have some understanding of the nature of right and wrong, that we be able to grasp the idea of what is meant by an act that is morally good or bad, that is to say, that our conscience be sufficiently developed and that, in the light of this conscience, we make our free choice. Such an act is called a moral act. Those people of whom we have just been speaking, although their understanding of right and wrong may in many cases be vague or faulty, have nevertheless sufficient understanding of this for a moral act; but young children have not, and therefore they are incapable as individuals of meriting an increase of sanctifying grace by their acts and therefore by their sufferings. Yet God permits them to take their share in the heritage of suffering common to the human race, and we cannot suppose that He lets them share in suffering as the penalty of Original Sin without also sharing in its merit as the instrument of Christ's redemptive act. Apart from the impossibility of reconciling such a supposition with God's goodness, power, and wisdom, it renders the inspired Scriptures meaningless when St. Paul, in words already quoted, says that "where sin [with suffering its effect] hath been multiplied, grace hath abounded yet more." How, then, can the sufferings of these little children merit a reward?

To solve this difficulty, we have to go still deeper into the doctrine of Christ's Mystical Body, for it is there, and there alone, that the answer lies. We have already seen that Christ and His Church (including both her visible and her invisible members, that is to say, all men whatsoever who are in the state of grace) form a single supernatural organism, Christ's Mystical Body, which St. Paul likens by analogy to the human body, Christ being the Head and the Church the members of the Body vivified by the Head, so that the Church united with Christ her Head forms with Him "one mystical Person," the "whole Christ." On Calvary, Christ merited superabundant grace for His Church and for all her members, so that the Church as a single mystical Person is able to draw upon the inexhaustible merits of her Head and thereby herself merit for and in those infant members of hers who are incapable as individuals of meriting for themselves. *She* acts meritoriously *in* them.

This is what happens in the sacrament of Baptism, which indeed is only fully understood in light of the Mystical Body. St. Thomas says, "Just as they [children at Baptism] believe *through the Church's faith,* so they desire the Eucharist *through the Church's intention,* and as a result receive its fruit [i.e., sanctifying grace]."[90] Heaven cannot be gained by anyone unless it is merited, yet an infant dying immediately after Baptism enters straight into Heaven. Has that infant merited Heaven by any moral act of his own will? No, because, as an individual, he is incapable of a moral act. Then who has merited Heaven for him? It is the Church who exercises faith *in* that child: "they believe through the Church's faith." In other words, the Church merits Heaven for that infant by her own faith exercised in this her little member and without any moral act on the child's part.

This may be illustrated by a case from nature. The human child before birth, while still in his mother's womb,

[90] *Summa Theologica,* III, Q. 73, art. 3.

although a distinct individual from her, does not nourish himself, nor is his blood circulated by the action of his own heart. It is the mother who nourishes the child by the circulation of *her own blood* through its body. *She* acts vitally in the unborn infant without any action on its own part as an individual. Only at birth does it exercise these functions of itself. So, too, does Mother Church perform her supernatural vital acts in those her little members who cannot as yet perform them for themselves.

Nor is this true only in the case of Baptism owing to its being a sacrament, because the Holy Innocents received sanctifying grace and gained Heaven, not only without any moral act on their part, but without receiving any sacrament either.[91] From this it follows conclusively that Christ can act in the infant members of His Mystical Body in other cases than the sacrament of Baptism — as by analogy *I* can act *in* my hands and feet — and, by His merits won on behalf of His Mystical Body and all its members, endow them with sanctifying grace. And this

---

[91] They received grace *by virtue of* the sacrament of Baptism, since without Baptism it is impossible to be "born again" into the supernatural state of grace (John 3:5), but without actually receiving the sacrament itself as such.

same principle underlies all the sufferings of infants and young children, since, as has already been said, Christ's use of suffering on Calvary as the instrument of His act of redemption has given to all human suffering whatsoever a quasi-sacramental value. If He could suffer in the Holy Innocents without any moral act on their part so as to produce in them their initial sanctifying grace, He can suffer in like manner in all children, likewise without any moral act on their part, so as to produce in them, if not their initial sanctifying grace, at least an increase thereof.

As the Church exercises faith meritoriously in the child as her member at Baptism, so, by reason of her union with Christ her Head, does she suffer meritoriously in the child. For her sufferings and the sufferings of all her members are a continuation of and draw all their value from the sufferings of her Head, which cannot be anything but meritorious. To suffer as Christ did in His Passion is an act of supreme supernatural charity, and since the Church forms "one mystical Person" with Him, she suffers as He did with the same charity that she has from Him by the Holy Spirit. When, therefore, she suffers in her infant members she produces in them the same supernatural charity with which her Head has suffered, and therefore an increase of sanctifying grace, the fruit of which is unending glory and bliss in Heaven.

Thus, speaking of children and of those who are on a par with children by reason of their irresponsibility due to insanity, mental deficiency, melancholia, and the like, Msgr. Benson says:

> Now, if you treat these cases as individual, if you regard the child as merely a complete entity in himself, the thing is and always must be inexplicable. Again and again we find ourselves asking, why should he suffer? He is not a Carmelite who understands; he is not a sinner to be reformed by discipline.
>
> But if you reflect that humanity as a whole is a great organism, used by God as the Body of His Passion[92] and that in the sufferings of this Body He carries out, on the mystical plane, His Redemption . . . and that this child is one cell of the Body of pain; you are no more intellectually puzzled as to

---

[92] Cf. Leo XIII, in the encyclical *Octobri mense:* "The eternal Son of God wished to assume human nature in order to redeem it. To do this, He had to consummate a mystic union with the *entire human race*."

why this child should suffer in particular than you are intellectually puzzled as to why your finger should ache instead of yourself. Your finger does not ache instead of yourself: you ache in your finger. This child does not suffer instead of humanity; but humanity suffers in him, and Christ therefore in him.

If, in short, you will insist upon treating each unit only as a unit (which is, in a word, Protestantism), you will never be satisfied; but if you understand that these units are more than units — they are cells in a Body — and if further you understand that it is Jesus Christ who lives and acts in this Body, that He truly therefore identifies Himself with every one of His members, a host of difficulties becomes luminous.[93]

If we turn back fifteen centuries, we can listen to St. Augustine saying the same thing: "Christ's whole Body groans with pain. Until the end of the world, when pain will pass away, this Man groans and cries to God. And each of us has part in the cry of that whole Body. Thou

[93] *Christ in the Church*, 188-189.

didst cry out in thy day, and thy days have passed away; another took thy place and cried out in his day. Thou here, he there, and another there. The Body of Christ ceases not to cry out all the day, one member replacing the other whose voice is hushed. Thus, there is but one Man who reaches unto the end of time, and those who cry are always His members."[94]

Christ, then, suffers through the centuries even in those members, the great majority, who do not themselves understand the meaning and merit of their pain, in those even who can in no way merit for themselves. With a strong hand, He has set His grasp upon suffering itself, the penalty of sin, universally and in all its forms, making of it an instrument by means of which man can merit a higher bliss in Heaven than ever he could have done had there been no sin and suffering. Christ did not destroy this terrible offspring of sin, but with infinitely greater power and wisdom, with greater generosity and love for us, has used it universally as a means of drawing from evil an immeasurably greater good for man.

---

[94] *In Psalm* 85. Cf. Emile Mersch, S.J., *The Whole Christ*, trans. John R. Kelly, S.J. (Bruce Publishing Company, 1938), 423.

The good use of suffering brings a reward

How many "useless" lives may be the most precious in God's sight! St. Benedict Joseph Labre[95] was a tramp, and a *very* dirty one. In him we understand how some of life's most hopeless failures may appear to God. This is no commendation of a morbid hankering after suffering, of slipshod methods and inefficiency. For it is God, not we, who plans the share of each. Our part is a *good use* of suffering when it comes. God is the husbandman, the human race the fertile soil from which He raises a harvest so rich in everlasting glory precisely because He has manured it and plowed it in with suffering.

꙾

Accepting God's will in all things brings
peace in this life and greater glory in Heaven

"If there could possibly be any envy in the kingdom of eternal love," says St. Francis de Sales,[96] "the angels would envy man for two privileges, which consist of two sufferings: the one is that which our Lord endured on the Cross for us, and not for them. . . . The other is that which men

---

[95] St. Benedict Joseph Labre (1748-1783), pilgrim and mendicant saint.

[96] St. Francis de Sales (1567-1622), Bishop of Geneva.

endure for our Lord; the suffering of God for man, the suffering of man for God." In the Mass, the angels are indeed privileged to partake in what is *our* sacrifice. In suffering, they have no such share; it is man's exclusive privilege.

To speak humanly, the smallest pain wrings God's heart more than the heart of any mother, yet even so, He permits it as the father permits his son's wounds in battle. Is the father cruel? The mere thought is preposterous. It is precisely because he *loves* his son and country that he takes pride in those very wounds which pierce his own heart. Thus did God permit the sufferings of Christ for our fallen race. Thus does He permit the sufferings of us who are Christ's members, who share His own redemptive work. For since it was by suffering that Christ redeemed mankind, He has by His Passion sanctified suffering for all time, giving to all suffering borne for love of Him a vast merit that exceeds our present understanding: "For I reckon that the sufferings of this time are not worthy to be compared with the glory to come that shall be revealed in us."[97] Can we then wonder that some, and maybe countless souls, will be raised by grace among the highest angels? "But we see Jesus, who was made a little lower than

[97] Rom. 8:18.

the angels, *for the suffering of death* crowned with glory and honor."[98] This high place among the angels in glory is offered to man, first, because he is Christ's own member, and, second, because he is a suffering member — *"for which cause* God also hath exalted him."[99] The more our life conforms to Christ's own life on earth, the closer are we "oned" with Him, the more fully do we cooperate in His own redemptive work for the salvation of souls, and the richer will be our share in His own glory in a life that has no end.

Christ has quite clearly foretold everything that is happening in the world today: "And you shall hear of wars and rumors of wars. See that ye be not troubled. For these things must come to pass; but the end is not yet. For nation shall rise against nation, and kingdom against kingdom; and there shall be pestilences and famines and earthquakes in places."[100] These are the words of Him who is infinite mercy and compassion! They are the words of Incarnate Wisdom, and He says, "See that ye be not troubled." Can anyone feel anything but troubled in the face

[98] Heb. 2:9.
[99] Phil. 2:9.
[100] Matt. 24:6-7.

of widespread slaughter of even defenseless populations by land, sea, and air, of invasion and the threat of tyrannical domination, of barbarous cruelties committed, of all the social upheavals and perhaps revolutions that follow upon war, and to all this the added anxiety over the fate of one's children in all the turmoil of an unknown future? Christ foresaw all this in its most minute detail since He is God, He understood perfectly all that men will suffer, and yet He says, "See that ye be not troubled," and no word of His can be empty or impossible of fulfillment.

It is true we cannot help *feeling* anxiety, trouble and fear, and perhaps feeling it intensely; if we did not, we would no longer be suffering, and Christ did not promise escape from suffering. But all this is in the lower part of our souls, in the emotions and feelings, and Christ is speaking of that higher or deeper part of the soul, its spiritual part, the understanding and the will, where deep-rooted peace can go hand in hand with the most intense suffering in the feelings, as it did with Christ Himself on Calvary, where in the utter and complete desolation of His feelings, He sent forth that dreadful cry: "My God, my God, why hast Thou forsaken me?"[101] Yet all the while, in

[101]Matt. 27:46.

the higher part of His soul, He possessed unbroken the blessed vision of the Godhead and perfect peace, that peace which He has promised to us if we will but fulfill the conditions for accepting it: "Peace I leave with you, my peace I give unto you; not as the world giveth, do I give unto you. Let not your heart be troubled, nor let it be afraid."[102] Not as the world gives, He says, because the peace that the world seeks to give is absence of suffering, but the peace of Christ is something immeasurably greater and deeper, for it can persist throughout all suffering, however grievous this may be.

And what is the condition of this peace? It consists in the "oneing" of our wills with the will of God, in that and nothing else; and let us remember that if we are honestly *trying* to unite our wills with God's will in all that happens to us, we are actually doing so, however much our feelings may still loathe the very suffering that our wills accept for the love of God. Did not Christ's whole emotional nature in Gethsemane shrink at the prospect of His Passion with a fear that has never been equaled, with a fear so intense that it forced the blood through the pores of His skin, *at the very time* when, with His free will, He was making the

[102]John 14:27.

most perfect act of accepting God's will that has ever been made? "My Father, if it be possible, let this chalice pass from me. Nevertheless, not as I will but as Thou wilt."[103]

So long as we merely seek escape from suffering, we shall never be at rest, but if, through all our sufferings, we seek God's will, we shall possess that deep-rooted peace which is Christ's gift to those who take Him at His word and trust Him absolutely, and no trial is so severe that we cannot do this by the grace of God. For no evil whatsoever happens save by God's permissive will; both we and our children are completely in His hands. "Fear ye not them that kill the body and are not able to kill the soul, but rather fear Him that can destroy both soul and body in Hell. Are not two sparrows sold for a farthing? And not one of them shall fall on the ground without your Father. But the very hairs of your head are all numbered. Fear not, therefore; better are you than many sparrows."[104]

Do we fear what may befall our children if we are taken? And cannot God take care of them as well as we can? But perhaps they will have to suffer terribly and lose all they would have had: education, position in life, liberty, and all

[103]Matt. 26:39.
[104]Matt. 10:28-31.

the rest? But are these the things that really matter ultimately? God has set us in this world as an antechamber to eternity, a temporary place of probation, nothing more than that; it is our salvation that really matters, and God has all that in His hands. Entrust all to Him whatever befall, trust Him *absolutely* because He is God without whom no man can move hand or foot nor wink an eyelid, and you shall have peace. It is from trusting almost exclusively in ourselves and not in God that restlessness of the will results, and it is precisely this restlessness that constitutes the worst part of our suffering. "Be you humbled, therefore, under the mighty hand of God," says St. Peter in his first letter, "that He may exalt you in the time of visitation; casting all your care on Him, for He hath care of you. . . . But the God of all grace, who hath called us unto His eternal glory in Christ Jesus, after you have suffered a little, will Himself perfect you and confirm you and establish you."[105]

The principle of the *felix culpa* is always at our disposal if we will but use it; so pleasing to God is an act of complete abandonment to His will in all things, and so sanctifying, that such an act made now to the best of our ability,

[105] 1 Pet. 5:6-7, 10.

if pursued as a habitual attitude of our will in spite of many failures to maintain it, can make up, and far more than make up, for all our ill use of God's graces in the past.

By every increase of sanctifying grace we are more perfectly incorporated into Christ, built up more fully into Him; and the more we are built up into His own Mystical Body, the more closely we are identified with Him, and the more fully do we share in the elevation of His own sacred humanity above all creation. And every suffering, since Christ has made of it a quasi-sacrament, is a channel of the superabundantly generous grace of redemption, and so, if accepted with good will, increases our incorporation in Christ and therefore our participation in the elevation of His own humanity. And in proportion as we participate in His own elevation as man above all created being shall we ourselves be raised for all eternity higher in the angelic hierarchy, increasing beyond anything we can conceive our glory and bliss in the everlasting vision of God. Could we but realize what even the smallest increase of glory is, we would understand St. Paul when he says that our present sufferings cannot so much as be measured against their everlasting reward, which, if we persevere to the end, will be ours as members of Christ's glorified Mystical Body in Heaven through all eternity.

The good use of suffering brings a reward

Let us, then, make use of almost the last words of Dame Julian to tell why God has left us suffering: "Wouldst thou witten thy Lord's meaning in this thing? Wit it well: Love was His meaning."

*

God awaits your response

The words of Dame Julian, quoted at the end of the previous chapter, drive to the root of the whole question: Love.

There is no place in Catholic theology for the "worship of suffering." The fanatical cult of Indian fakirs is as far removed from the Christian spirit as is the modern horror of suffering that seeks escape at any cost.

The Church regards human suffering with an immense reverence, for she sees in it the redemptive Passion of her Head carried on throughout time. But nothing can compare with the compassion she shows toward all who suffer, as is evident from the ministrations of those countless religious women whose lives are wholly devoted to its relief, a work that reflects through the ages the infinite compassion displayed in every one of Christ's own miracles.

Why Does God Permit Evil?

In itself, suffering is indifferent either to moral good or to moral evil. It is the use that is made of it that matters. Both thieves on Calvary underwent the same suffering, yet with what different results! Suffering ill-borne causes rankle in the soul, while suffering sought for its own sake merely produces pride.

How, then, does suffering sanctify? And in what does holiness consist? There are mistaken notions of holiness not together uncommon that regard it as the monopoly of some special class. If holiness is this, then clearly it is impossible for the ordinary man. Yet if we are members of Christ, how can we say we are not called to holiness? Can Christ's own living members be anything but holy, unless they are not all that grace intended them to be?

The word *holy* is derived from the Old English *hal,* as are *hale* and *whole,* and all alike mean "sound" or "complete," just as the Latin derivative *perfect,* from *per* and *facere,* means "something carried through to its full development." Holiness is the wholeness, the full growth, the complete development of baptismal grace, whether this be given by the actual reception of the sacrament itself or, in the case of invincible ignorance, by Baptism of desire. "So is the kingdom of God, as if a man should cast seed into the earth . . . and the seed should spring and grow up . . . first the blade, then the ear, afterward the full corn in the ear."[106] Manure is indeed indispensable for a rich harvest, yet the vital origin of the harvest is the seed. It is as essential to the nature of baptismal grace to grow as it is for a grain of wheat to produce the ripened corn, granting that the conditions of growth are not impeded. For God continuously supplies actual graces that are to the baptized soul as sunlight and rain to the growing corn.

God, therefore, would contradict His wisdom if He gave baptismal grace and refused the actual graces necessary for the fullness of its growth. By Baptism man becomes Christ's own member, and that is already essential holiness. But each member or cell in a living organism is made to attain full growth. Hence, everyone, no matter how unfavorable the circumstances of his life may appear to be, is called to holiness of some kind and degree.

But the holiness of each is different. There are many tissues in the human body, and even within the same tissue, no two cells are quite the same. It is the stranger, not the shepherd, who thinks all sheep in the flock are alike. God's music is not ended with one tune. The beauty of "the whole Christ" demands this variety, for beauty is

[106]Mark 4:26-28.

variety centered in unity. Unity alone is monotony, the prolonged sounding of a single note. Variety alone is chaos. The unity is that of Christ's Mystical Body, the variety that of its tissues and cells. So the dignity of each one's vocation consists, not in being higher than another, but in being unique, formed by God to fulfill its own function in Christ's Body, which no other can ever fulfill. God does not intend miraculous graces or canonization save for a few, and many a hidden soul whom no one so much as suspected of sanctity while on earth may be among the greatest saints without either. But He does intend that the graces offered to each should reach their full maturity, and He suits His graces to the circumstances of each, however bad these appear to be. Let us put it this way: fifty talents ill used may produce fifty-five, and two talents well used, four. The latter is holiness, the former is not. The former is indeed a call to higher holiness, but it has not been reached. The latter is to lesser holiness, yet it has been attained.

༄

Suffering must be borne with love
Yet, while each one's holiness is unique, the essential activity in which all holiness whatsoever consists is one.

It is love. Suffering can be practiced from a motive of pride, as in the case of many a self-chosen penance; it is only as the expression of love for God that it sanctifies. The test comes when we are faced with some unexpected trial in which we ourselves had no choice. How often some pious person who revels in self-chosen mortifications rebels as soon as he or she is faced with such a trial coming from the hands of God. The former enshrined a large measure of self-will; the latter, the pure will of God. This is the test that sifts out mere piety from solid holiness. Fasting is good, yet better by far to suffer with patience the irritating ways of others than to fast and snap at one's neighbor, since it is charity that is the live current that gives to penance its whole power for good. "A person who suffers martyrdom with one ounce of love," says St. Francis de Sales, merits much, for one cannot give more than one's life, yet another person who suffers no more than a fillip, but does so with two ounces of love, will have more merit, because it is charity and love which give all things their value."

Yet *love* is a dangerous word, for we are so prone to think of it as emotional experience. "I have noticed in all our houses," St. Francis de Sales said to his nuns, "that our sisters do not make a distinction between God and the feeling of God, between faith and the feeling of faith; which is a very great fault and an indication of ignorance." When nerves are tired, we may have no experience of love, no relish or interest. But love essentially is not an emotion. Let us leave the emotions to come and go; they matter little. "A single act performed with dryness of soul is worth more," he says elsewhere, "than several that are accompanied with great unction, because it is done with a stronger love, although it is not so emotional or so agreeable."

Love lies in the will. The word *devotion* has been sentimentalized. St. Thomas defines it as "the *will* to give oneself readily to things concerning the service of God."[107] Love is the "oneing" of the human will by obedience with the will of God, of which we have the most perfect example in Gethsemane, where the accompanying emotion was not of love, but of fear. Suffering can indeed destroy the *feeling* of love, but it purifies and strengthens love in the will, thus increasing its merit. In this obedience consisted the holiness of Christ as man: "I came not to do my own will, but the will of Him who sent me."[108] Such, too,

[107]*Summa Theologica*, II-II, Q. 82, art. 1.
[108]John 6:38.

144

is the holiness of all the saints, such is our own, since all they did and all we do is holy only insofar as it fulfills the will of God.

"Holiness may be reduced to one point only," says Père de Caussade, "fidelity to the order of God. . . . There is nothing so easy, so common, so constantly present in the hands of all as sanctity. . . . Just as the good and the bad thief had not different things to do and to suffer in order to be saints, so two souls, one worldly and the other all interior and spiritual, have nothing more, one than the other, to do and suffer. . . . The heart alone makes the difference between them. . . . By the heart is meant the will. Sanctity consists in *willing* what happens to us by God's order. What can be easier?"[109]

But to do this means for us, as for Christ Himself, the acceptance of suffering that is inseparable from the sinful condition of our race. Why suffering is so sanctifying if accepted for love of God is, first, as has already been said, because Christ has sanctified suffering by His Passion, giving it a quasi-sacramental value; then also because it

---

[109]Jean-Pierre de Caussade, *Self-Abandonment to Divine Providence*, Algar Thorold, trans. (London: Burns, Oates, and Washbourne), 6, 23-24.

purifies and intensifies our act of love. For to do God's will when this involves distaste and suffering means that our act can have little or no self-complacence mixed up with it, as may easily happen when we do something pleasant, even if it be for God. Like fire, it purges our love so that it is *all* for God. Even in ordinary life, we expect a return in proportion to the price we pay. The angels received glory in reward for a most pure act of love, yet it cost them no suffering. We pay the high price of suffering in order to do God's will, and God's response is immeasurably generous.

God arranges the character of our holiness. He provides the inborn temperament, and the circumstances in which we live. Our part consists in one continuous act, seeking His will in each event as it flows past on the stream of time. This does not mean sitting by and doing nothing while life glides past us, but the generous action of our will going out constantly to God.

The present event enshrining God's will for us may be pleasant or unpleasant. It is a great mistake to suppose God's will is always an unpleasant thing; let us thank Him for the sweets He sends us. Again, it may be something to accept, perhaps the death or ingratitude of a friend, the loss of property or good name, the patient bearing with our own faults. "To bear with oneself is an act of great virtue," says Fr. Considine, S.J.[110] Or it may be a call to action, a temptation to resist, to forgive, or to help another at real inconvenience to oneself, or maybe the fearless defense of Christian principles and rights. By thus keeping our eyes upon each passing event as enshrining God's will for us, we shall accept just that measure of suffering, no more and no less, which providence sees to be good for each of us.

For every event is — in a wide and analogous sense — a sacrament; it is the external sign containing within it God's action upon us, and, like the water of Baptism or the bread and wine of the Eucharist, all of which are such common and ordinary materials, these events are mostly very ordinary and unromantic, for God loves to use the commonplace things of life for high supernatural ends.

There was nothing romantic about the little shop at Nazareth, and in our own lives, there is little romance about cooking meals, mending clothes, or keeping the ledger.

[110]*Words of Encouragement* (pamphlet of the Catholic Truth Society).

Why Does God Permit Evil?

⚜

God desires your yes

We are free to disregard God's action on us or to accept it. If we say yes, the divine action finds entry to the soul in a communion most close and sanctifying. Life is a continuous sacrament; it can become a perpetual Communion. As sunlight floods the surface of the earth, being held back only by an upturned stone, so is God's action a continuous stream of grace resisted only by the malice of the human will. It is always the event of the present moment that forms, as it were, the sacramental "species within which lies hidden, intensely active, God's will, and that is God Himself."

Père de Caussade calls this "the Sacrament of the Present Moment." "What happens to us at each moment by God's order," he says, "is precisely what for us is the holiest, the best, the most divine thing that could happen. . . . The present moment is always full of infinite treasures; it contains far more than you have the capacity to hold. The Divine Will is an abyss, the opening of which is the present moment."

On a summer day, a flower opens wide its petals, exposing its whole face to the sun. The sun's rays flow in and build up its tissues. Such is the soul that opens wide to

God's action, allowing grace to enter in and its fabric to grow. Some people are too busy about themselves; they turn inward like flowers closed up. Let us turn Godward. It is His work. Our part is to open wide, to say yes, to avoid cramping the divine action. The little boy who holds the handles of the wheelbarrow he can scarcely lift shouts with glee as he toddles on, and his father who does all the work delights to hear him. So does our heavenly Father love to see our good will, although it is all the doing of His grace. He does the entire work of transforming us into Christ, provided we allow Him to do it by saying yes to all He does.

The Incarnation depended, in one sense, wholly on our Lady's yes, for she was free. St. Bernard[111] has a dramatic passage in which he pictures all creation in suspense for her answer: "Be it done to me according to thy word."[112] Yet it was entirely God's work, and the greatness of it was beyond all proportion to our Lady's act. In like manner, our transformation into Christ is dependent altogether upon our continuous yes, yet from start to finish, it is God's work. In this work also the fruit is great, wholly

[111]St. Bernard of Clairvaux (1090-1153), abbot and Doctor.
[112]Luke 1:38.

surpassing the littleness of our acts; it is proportionate to the grace that at each moment God offers us. Graces differ for each soul, yet the least grace is so precious that we cannot attempt to understand it now.

In his life of the Curé d'Ars, the Abbé Francis Trochu relates how in the year 1856, a lady found herself by chance at Ars. She was desperate, for her husband, after abandoning his Faith, had drowned himself, and she could not doubt that he had lost his soul. She took her place with the crowd that gathered each day between the church and the presbytery as the holy Curé came from his morning catechism. He had never met her, nor ever heard of her. He stopped and whispered in her ear, "He is saved." He repeated it, but still she was incredulous. "I tell you he is saved," he insisted, stressing each word. "Between the parapet of the bridge and the water, he had time to make an act of contrition."

The reward of divine mercy for the last momentary act of that man's life was the Vision of God forever. Now, every act we make in the state of grace increases our capital of grace, so that successive acts, outwardly the same, become continuously of greater merit since they spring from a higher capital — that is, from a higher state of charity in the soul, as an interest of five percent on a thousand pounds produces more than the same interest on a hundred. What, then, must be the reward for a lifetime spent in doing the divine will? God hides the reward from us now; otherwise life on earth would be insupportable.

By thus seeking God's will in all that happens, joyful or sorrowful, in failure or success, we must necessarily always find that which we are looking for. God's will is always there. Holiness is for all; it is simple. Hear the master of spirituality Jean-Pierre Caussade: "O all you who . . . are tempted to discouragement at the sight of what you read in the lives of the saints and what is prescribed in certain pious books . . . it is for your consolation that God wishes me to write this."

Yes, *whoever you may be* who are reading this, you can become holy by seeking God in the humdrum things of your daily life and in the sufferings it brings to you. However monotonous or difficult may be the events that go to make up your life, even if at times they present themselves as trials that test your endurance and fortitude to the utmost, God is in each of them, and He is there to make a saint of you if you give Him the chance.

By seeking God in all things, we come at length to see Him at all times, not with the open vision of glory, but by faith, as through a veil, living ever in His presence. This

Why Does God Permit Evil?

means peace of soul and joy solidly founded in the will. Our emotions come and go, but whatever they may be, peace remains. The surface of the ocean may be storm-tossed, but in its deep waters, there is always calm. We may lose what we prized so much, we may feel crushed by some trial, yet we retain our deep-set joy, for in the light of our Catholic Faith, we know the meaning of these trials.

Thank God our religion is one of triumph.

The predominant note of the Church's heroic soul is joy. While the world is becoming desperately intent on everything but God, the Church is merry with the joy of Christ and nothing can quench her irrepressible gaiety. She never forgets her joy even during her seasons of penance; on Good Friday her Liturgy rings with this majestic note: "Behold through the wood of the Cross joy is come into all the world." There are times when her Alleluias have the rhythm of a dance. England was proverbially merry when she was Catholic. Intensely Catholic is the gaiety of an Irish Jig. It is only a neopagan world that is forgetting how to laugh.

This joy, the hallmark of holiness, can be ours, because we know the vast treasures that lie hidden within the event of each passing moment and the supernatural wealth of suffering. Each moment holds a grace that can blossom into eternal glory beyond our understanding now. The longest life is but a passing moment. We stand on the brink of eternity: "Behold I come quickly and my reward is with me, to render to each according to his work. . . . Yea, I come quickly." Amen. Come, Lord Jesus."[113]

[113]Cf. Apoc. 22:12, 20 (RSV = Rev. 22:12, 20).

Sophia Institute

Sophia Institute is a nonprofit institution that seeks to nurture the spiritual, moral, and cultural life of souls and to spread the Gospel of Christ in conformity with the authentic teachings of the Roman Catholic Church.

Sophia Institute Press fulfills this mission by offering translations, reprints, and new publications that afford readers a rich source of the enduring wisdom of mankind.

Sophia Institute also operates two popular online Catholic resources: CrisisMagazine.com and CatholicExchange.com.

Crisis Magazine provides insightful cultural analysis that arms readers with the arguments necessary for navigating the ideological and theological minefields of the day. *Catholic Exchange* provides world news from a Catholic perspective as well as daily devotionals and articles that will help you to grow in holiness and live a life consistent with the teachings of the Church.

In 2013, Sophia Institute launched Sophia Institute for Teachers to renew and rebuild Catholic culture through service to Catholic education. With the goal of nurturing the spiritual, moral, and cultural life of souls, and an abiding respect for the role and work of teachers, we strive to provide materials and programs that are at once enlightening to the mind and ennobling to the heart; faithful and complete, as well as useful and practical.

Sophia Institute gratefully recognizes the Solidarity Association for preserving and encouraging the growth of our apostolate over the course of many years. Without their generous and timely support, this book would not be in your hands.

www.SophiaInstitute.com
www.CatholicExchange.com
www.CrisisMagazine.com
www.SophiaInstituteforTeachers.org

Sophia Institute Press® is a registered trademark of Sophia Institute.
Sophia Institute is a tax-exempt institution as defined by the
Internal Revenue Code, Section 501(c)(3). Tax I.D. 22-2548708.